FISCAL FEDERALISM
AND EQUALIZATION
POLICY IN CANADA

The Johnson-Shoyama Series on Public Policy

Taking a comparative and international perspective, the Johnson-Shoyama Series on Public Policy focuses on the many approaches to major policy issues offered by Canada's provinces and territories and reflected in their intergovernmental relationships. Books in the series each explore particular policy issues, and while research-based, are intended to engage informed readers and students alike.

FISCAL FEDERALISM AND EQUALIZATION POLICY IN CANADA

Political and Economic Dimensions

Daniel Béland
(Johnson-Shoyama Graduate School of Public Policy)

André Lecours
(University of Ottawa)

Gregory P. Marchildon
(University of Toronto)

Haizhen Mou
(Johnson-Shoyama Graduate School of Public Policy)

M. Rose Olfert
(Johnson-Shoyama Graduate School of Public Policy)

 UNIVERSITY OF TORONTO PRESS

LIBRARY AND ARCHIVES CANADA CATALOGUING IN PUBLICATION

Lecours, André, 1972–, author Fiscal federalism and equalization policy in Canada : political and economic dimensions / Daniel Béland (Johnson-Shoyama Graduate School of Public Policy), André Lecours (University of Ottawa), Gregory P. Marchildon (University of Toronto), Haizhen Mou (Johnson-Shoyama Graduate School of Public Policy), M. Rose Olfert (Johnson-Shoyama Graduate School of Public Policy).

(The Johnson-Shoyama series on public policy)

Includes bibliographical references and index.

Issued in print and electronic formats.

ISBN 978-1-4426-3541-8 (softcover).—ISBN 978-1-4426-3542-5 (hardcover).—ISBN 978-1-4426-3543-2 (HTML).—ISBN 978-1-4426-3544-9 (PDF)

1. Transfer payments—Canada. 2. Federal government—Canada. 3. Canada—Economic policy. I. Marchildon, Gregory P., 1956–, author II. Olfert, M.R. (Margaret Rose), 1950–, author III. Béland, Daniel, author V. Mou, Haizhen, 1977–, author V. Title. VI. Series: Johnson-Shoyama series on public policy

HJ795.A1L43 2017   336.1'850971   C2017-900694-0
                                                C2017-900695-9

We welcome comments and suggestions regarding any aspect of our publications—please feel free to contact us at news@utphighereducation.com or visit our Internet site at www.utppublishing.com.

North America
5201 Dufferin Street
North York, Ontario, Canada, M3H 5T8

2250 Military Road
Tonawanda, New York, USA, 14150

ORDERS PHONE: 1-800-565-9523
ORDERS FAX: 1-800-221-9985
ORDERS E-MAIL: utpbooks@utpress.utoronto.ca

UK, Ireland, and continental Europe
NBN International
Estover Road, Plymouth, PL6 7PY, UK
ORDERS PHONE: 44 (0) 1752 202301
ORDERS FAX: 44 (0) 1752 202333
ORDERS E-MAIL: enquiries@nbninternational.com

This book is printed on paper containing 100% post-consumer fibre.

The University of Toronto Press acknowledges the financial support for its publishing activities of the Government of Canada through the Canada Book Fund.

Printed in the United States of America.

Contents

Illustrations

Figures

Tables

Acknowledgements

The authors thank Rachel Hatcher for her copy-editing support, Colten Goertz and Ebrahim Hassanpourand for their research assistance, David Péloquin for his detailed comments, and the anonymous reviewers for their suggestions. Special thanks to Mat Buntin, Michael Harrison, and the rest of the University of Toronto Press team for their excellent work. Daniel Béland and André Lecours acknowledge support from the Social Sciences and Humanities Research Council of Canada. Daniel Béland also receives funding from the Canada Research Chairs Program. Finally, thank you to the Johnson-Shoyama Graduate School of Public Policy for supporting the publication of this book and, more generally, the Johnson-Shoyama Series on Public Policy at the University of Toronto Press.

The Authors

Daniel Béland is a professor and Canada Research Chair in Public Policy (Tier 1) at the Johnson-Shoyama Graduate School of Public Policy. A student of comparative social and fiscal policy, he has published 14 books and more than 100 articles in peer-reviewed journals. Written with André Lecours, his articles on equalization policy have appeared in *Publius, Journal of Public Policy*, and *Canadian Journal of Political Science*. Recent books include *Obamacare Wars* (University Press of Kansas, 2016; with Philip Rocco and Alex Waddan) and *Welfare Reform in Canada* (University of Toronto Press, 2015; co-edited with Pierre-Marc Daigneault).

André Lecours is a professor in the School of Political Studies at the University of Ottawa. He is a specialist of Canadian and comparative federalism, and he has taught and published extensively in that field. He is the editor of *New Institutionalism: Theory and Analysis*, published by the University of Toronto Press in 2005; the author of *Basque Nationalism and the Spanish State* (University of Nevada Press, 2007); and the co-author (with Daniel Béland) of *Nationalism and Social Policy: The Politics of Territorial Solidarity* (Oxford University Press, 2008). He has also published numerous book chapters and journal articles.

Gregory P. Marchildon is Ontario Research Chair in Health Policy and System Design at the Institute of Health Policy, Management and Evaluation, and Professor in the school of Public Policy and Governance, University of Toronto. As a former Deputy Minister of Intergovernmental Affairs and cabinet secretary in the Saskatchewan government and as the executive director of the Royal Commission on the Future of Health Care in Canada (the Romanow Commission), he has considerable federal-provincial relations experience with equalization and other federal transfers. Trained as an economist and historian, he has published over a hundred articles and book chapters on federalism and health care. His most recent books include *Bending the Cost Curve in Health Care* (University of Toronto Press, 2014), *Health Systems in Transition: Canada* (University of Toronto Press, 2013), and *Nunavut: A Health System Profile* (McGill-Queen's University Press, 2013).

Haizhen Mou is an associate professor at the Johnson-Shoyama Graduate School of Public Policy. An economist by training, her primary research interests include health care financing and expenditure, cost and efficiency of public sectors, and government budget management, often from a political economy perspective. She has published in *Canadian Journal of Economics, Canadian Public Policy, Public Finance Review*, and *Health Policy*.

M. Rose Olfert is a professor emerita at the Johnson-Shoyama Graduate School of Public Policy. A regional economist by training and practice, she has published widely on the determinants of differences in regional economic outcomes, focusing on the rural regions of North America. She has published more than 70 papers in refereed journals and book chapters. Her empirical work has appeared in *Public Finance Review, Journal of Economic Geography,* and *Regional Science and Urban Economics*. Public sector influences in regional economic development are an underlying theme in her work. She has also taught public finance at the graduate level.

Introduction

Most federal systems have developed stand-alone equalization programs to reduce fiscal inequalities among constituent units. In Canada, the federal equalization program is widely debated; redistributing large sums of money to less well-off provinces is always potentially controversial. In 2016–17, to fulfill its constitutional obligation, the federal government allocated more than $17.8 billion to six provinces that have a fiscal capacity below the equalization standard.[1] The program's importance to the recipient provinces and its redistributive nature make it a contentious political issue. Unprecedented territorial conflict over the equalization system during the Martin and early Harper years led to some key policy revisions. Although the political debate over equalization has calmed down considerably since then, the policy remains controversial. Provincial grievances as well as reform proposals, including changing the extent to which resource revenues are included in the formula, are regular issues in debates about the future of fiscal federalism in Canada.

In spite of the importance of equalization for citizens and governments alike, public knowledge about this federal program is sorely lacking. For instance, it is common to read that equalization is a direct transfer of fiscal resources from "have" to "have-not" provinces, a misleading representation of how the program works (Lecours and Béland 2010). Despite the outstanding work of economists such as Robin Boadway, Tom Courchene, and Anwar Shah, equalization remains a poorly understood program outside small expert circles. Moreover, the nature and workings of equalization are often distorted in both the media and political discourse. Furthermore, as changes have been made to the program, with more changes pending, current, accessible, and accurate information about equalization remains scant. The resulting lack of public understanding is related to the inner complexity of the program as well as the inflammatory rhetoric that surrounds it, a situation stemming at least in part from the size of the transfers and ongoing political struggles over power and influence.

---

1 Among the three major federal transfers to the provinces (equalization, Canada Health Transfer, and Canada Social Transfer), equalization is the second largest behind the Canada Health Transfer ($36 billion in 2016–17).

The objective of this concise book is to increase public understanding of equalization by providing a comparative and interdisciplinary perspective on the history, politics, and economics of equalization policy in Canada. The focus is on the federal equalization program created in 1957 and its relationship to public policy and provincial politics. Also included is a discussion of other components of Canadian fiscal federalism, especially the other largest federal transfers to the provinces: the Canada Health Transfer and the Canada Social Transfer. To explain to Canadians what equalization is and how it works, the book provides: a short history of the equalization program in comparative perspective; an analysis of the politics of equalization as witnessed over the last decade; a discussion of key economic debates about the role of the program and its effects; and, finally, an exploration of the relationship between equalization and fiscal federalism at large, particularly the Canada Health Transfer and the Canada Social Transfer.

This book offers an interdisciplinary perspective on equalization that draws from the best scholarship available in the fields of economics, economic history, political science, public policy, and comparative sociology. Most of the literature on equalization policy is dominated by the discipline of economics, and, although our book draws extensively on this rich material (two of the co-authors are economists by training), it also uses other approaches and disciplines to explore the political and policy aspects of equalization while placing it in a comparative, historical, and policy context.

The chapters

This book is divided into four chapters. The first chapter explores the emergence of equalization policy in Canada from an historical and comparative perspective. More particularly, it explains why Canada came to adopt a federal equalization program in 1957 in the context of the decline of the tax-rental agreements between Ottawa and the provinces, first signed during World War II. This chapter also discusses how the Canadian experience with equalization policy differs from that of other federal countries. One of the central goals of this comparative and historical chapter is to locate equalization within the broader context of the political and fiscal management of the federation. For instance, this chapter discusses the status of Québec within the Canadian federal system and the potential relationship between equalization and national unity issues. The last part of the chapter formulates a direct comparison between Australia and Canada. The objective of this discussion is to explain why Canada rejected two key aspects of the "Australian model" created in the early to mid-1930s: first, the creation of an arm's-length expert commission in charge of determining equalization payments and, second, the consideration of expenditure needs alongside fiscal capacity in the calculation of such payments. Overall, this chapter uses historical and comparative analysis to illuminate key policy choices that have shaped Canada's distinct equalization system.

The second chapter focuses on the politics of equalization during the Martin (2003–06) and Harper (2006–15) years. Paying close attention to the politics of equalization is especially important because most of the scholarship on equalization is undertaken by economists, who seldom analyze the politics of equalization in a systematic manner (on this issue, see Lecours and Béland 2010). As argued in this second chapter, at the most general level, the politicization of equalization in Canada is in large part the product of the program's governance structure, which is grounded in federal executive discretion. More specifically, four factors are particularly important in explaining why the federal equalization program became so politically contentious in the mid-2000s. First, increasing oil prices exacerbated political tensions over horizontal fiscal redistribution. Second, in a context of growing partisan competition in the aftermath of the unification of the right through the advent of the Conservative Party of Canada in 2003, executive discretion over the federal equalization program made it possible for federal politicians to attempt to use equalization for political gain. Third, strong existing provincial identities coupled with the willingness of premiers such as Danny Williams (Newfoundland and Labrador) to mobilize these identities against federal minority governments intensified intergovernmental tensions. Finally, public and media perceptions of the program added fuel to the fiery debates about equalization. After discussing these four factors in detail, the chapter concludes with a discussion of a possible reform of equalization governance aimed at potentially reducing future political conflict over the program.

The third chapter focuses on the economics of equalization. The starting point of this chapter is that the economic case for equalization payments arises from the recognition that the advantages of a decentralized form of government may be offset by regional differences that create perverse incentives. Ideally, the internal mobility of people and resources responds to economic incentives to produce the best national outcomes. However, constituent provinces may have very different endowments and thus very different potentials to provide public services to their populations. They might also have very different needs when it comes to taxing these populations. Provinces with an abundance of revenues, for example, may attract population (and labour) based on their ability to provide public goods and services; this migration is referred to as fiscally induced migration. This type of migration is undesirable in that it is not in the direction of higher productivity. One way to "correct for" or reduce fiscally induced migration is through the equalization of the revenue capacity of the provinces, which is the intent of Canada's equalization program. However, the economic literature suggests that, under some conditions, equalization payments may also create "welfare traps" in recipient provinces, removing the incentive for economic migration and making both the "trapped" population and the country worse off in the long run. After outlining the economic basis for equalization payments, this chapter explores the extent to which Canada's program has been successful in its economic objectives. Major challenges that remain are also discussed, such as the effectiveness of equalization payments in addressing inefficient migration, which revenue bases should be included in the assessment of provincial revenue capacity, the use of a moving average to calculate equalization entitlements, and the potential negative effects of equalization transfers.

The fourth chapter offers a broader perspective on fiscal federalism by looking at the relationship between the equalization program and the larger system of federal transfers to the provinces, in particular the Canada Health Transfer (CHT) and the Canada Social Transfer (CST), the two largest specific-purpose transfers. Although equalization is not the largest transfer (this claim to fame belongs to the CHT), it is the best known of the three transfers because of its longer history and its constitutional status. Equalizing transfers, however, are not limited to the Canadian Fiscal Equalization Program. Until recently, there were equalization components in the allocation formulas for the CHT and CST. However, the adoption of the equal per capita allocation (for CST starting in 2007 and for CHT starting in 2014) removed the equalizing dimension in these programs. As a result, lower-income provinces now have to rely more heavily on equalization payments to supplement own-source revenues to finance rapidly growing social expenditures, especially health care. Given the contested nature and history of equalization in Canada, there is room for the federal government to better coordinate the design of the three federal transfers to achieve their respective policy objectives. In this chapter, we first briefly review the purpose, history, and politics of the CHT and CST. We then link this review with the prior analysis of the equalization program to assess the performance of the three transfers as a group in achieving their objectives. We then discuss the advantage and disadvantage of using CHT to achieve the purpose of equalization, particularly in regards to addressing the different expenditure needs of the provinces, compared to the alternative of modifying the equalization program, which should be focused on differing revenue capacities.

The brief conclusion summarizes the main points made in the book before discussing potential reform scenarios regarding the future of equalization policy in Canada. Our conclusion shows that Canada cannot dismantle equalization altogether for economic, political, and constitutional reasons and stresses issues that Canadians should focus on when discussing the future of a crucial yet misunderstood and contentious federal program.

References

Béland, Daniel, and André Lecours. 2010. "Does Nationalism Trigger Welfare State Disintegration? Social Policy and Territorial Mobilization in Belgium and Canada." *Environment and Planning C: Government and Policy* 28 (3): 420–34.

Lecours, André, and Daniel Béland. 2010. "Federalism and Fiscal Policy: The Politics of Equalization in Canada." *Publius: The Journal of Federalism* 40 (4): 569–96. http://dx.doi.org/10.1093/publius/pjp030.

one

Equalization in Comparative and Historical Perspective

Introduction

Comparative and historical perspectives are important in the study of public policy because policies are the product of long-term economic and political processes that can vary greatly from country to country.[1] Reviewing historical processes within a comparative framework helps to explain key differences between countries. In the case of equalization policy in Canada, such an approach can shed light on the structure of the program as it developed in the post–World War II era.

This chapter explores the emergence and development of equalization policy in Canada from an historical and comparative perspective. After showing how the Canadian experience differs from that in other federal countries, the chapter explains why, in the context of the decline of the tax rental agreements that were first signed between Ottawa and the provinces during World War II, Canada came to adopt a federal equalization program in 1957.

One of the central objectives of this chapter is to locate equalization within the broader political and fiscal context of federalism, in Canada and in other federal systems. We discuss, for example, the status of Québec within the Canadian federal system and the potential relationship between equalization and national unity. Another key aspect of the chapter concerns the choice of the governance model adopted for equalization policy in 1957, in contrast to the model developed in Australia during the early and mid-1930s. This "Australian model," which features an arm's-length expert commission in charge of determining equalization payments, was explicitly rejected in Canada in 1957, as was the idea that expenditure needs should be considered alongside fiscal capacity to calculate equalization payments, in contrast, expenditure needs were part of the calculation in Australia. To better explain the choices made about the nascent equalization program in Canada, we provide, toward the end of the chapter, a comparison between it and Australia's equalization policy.

---

1 The first and the last main sections of this chapter draw directly on Béland and Lecours (2016).

From fiscal federalism to equalization policy

In Canada, equalization policy is a key component of modern fiscal federalism, that is, of how federal fiscal resources are redistributed among different levels of government. The basis of fiscal federalism is the "redistribution of revenue" between central and constituent unit governments (Watts 2008, 95). In most federal systems, as Ronald Watts (2008) notes, the central government is allocated substantial taxation powers as a way to mitigate fiscal competition among constituent units and to draw on "the *administrative* advantages of centralizing certain kinds of revenue levying and tax collection" (95). As a result, all federations witness a fiscal gap "between the revenues and expenditures of central governments and constituent units, and every central government transfers funds to the constituent units. Through such transfers, central governments exercise their spending power to achieve various goals, including national standards and objectives" (Atkinson et al. 2013, 10).[2] The centralization of taxation powers is never absolute, however, as constituent units must have the capacity to generate some own-source revenues in order for their constitutional powers to translate to the policy level.

The constitutional division of taxation powers between the central and constituent unit governments varies greatly across federal systems. Looking at central government revenues as a percentage of total government revenues before intergovernmental transfers provides a perspective on fiscal centralization in federal systems (see Table 1.1).

This indicator suggests that Canada is, from a fiscal perspective, is a most fiscally-decentralized federation, with less than half of total government revenues originating at the federal level. Other centralization indicators suggest a similar conclusion. For example, provincial governments have very few restrictions on their own-source revenues, and their borrowing autonomy is unconstrained. Provincial governments have access to major tax revenue sources such as income tax and sales tax. Also, Canadian provinces are not highly reliant on federal transfers in comparison with constituent units in other federal systems (see Table 1.2).[3]

Another indicator of the levels of fiscal centralization of federations is the conditionality of transfers. In Canada, the two main vertical transfers, the Canada Health Transfer (CHT) and the Canada Social Transfer

---

2 For a discussion of the concept of spending power in comparative perspective, see Watts (1999).

3 OECD data for Australia under this category are currently unavailable.

Table 1.1 Federal government tax revenues as a percentage of total government revenues in six OECD federal countries, 2013

Australia	80.8
Mexico	80.1
Belgium	57.1
Canada	41.6
United States	41.2
Switzerland	35.2

Source: OECD.

Table 1.2 Intergovernmental transfers as a percentage of constituent unit total revenue in five OECD federal countries, 2014

Mexico	70 (2013)
Belgium	64.5
Switzerland	25.1
United States	18.9
Canada	18.8

Source: OECD.

(CST), come with conditions that are not overly constraining. To receive the CST, provinces cannot impose a minimum residency requirement for residents to receive social assistance. As for the CHT, the federal government has the right to reduce transfers to specific provinces by a discretionary amount if it judges that such provinces do not respect the five criteria (portability, accessibility, universality, comprehensiveness, and public administration) or if they allow user fees or extra billing as specified in the 1984 Canada Health Act. Nevertheless, overall, one can say that Canadian provinces enjoy strong fiscal autonomy and that, as a consequence, they can pursue their own policy objectives within their areas of jurisdiction (Atkinson et al. 2013).

While Canadian provinces have one of the highest degrees of policy autonomy compared to constituent units of other federations, the federal government is preeminent in several policy fields (criminal justice, international relations, currency, defence, and citizenship). Provinces play a significant, though shared, role in many other crucial fields (social policy, transportation, agriculture, language, culture, financial regulation, and the environment). In yet other key policy fields (education, health care, employment relations, civil law, natural resources, and policing), provinces have the dominant policy-making position.

These remarks about the high level of fiscal decentralization and provincial autonomy should not obscure the fact that political and policy debates in Canada feature two types of fiscal gap. The first is a vertical fiscal gap, which typically refers to the claim "that the federal government's tax sources are much greater than its expenditure responsibilities whereas, in the provinces, precisely the opposite is the case" (Atkinson et al. 2013, 62). Another term used in academic and political discourse to describe the vertical fiscal gap is fiscal imbalance, which typically refers to the claim that, given the fiscal gap and limited federal transfers, provincial total revenues do not increase rapidly enough to keep pace with growing policy expenditures. Politically, the claim that Canada is characterized by a vertical fiscal imbalance has been used by provincial leaders to seek greater fiscal transfers from Ottawa. This is particularly the case in Québec, a province that has long articulated a strong discourse denouncing vertical fiscal imbalance in Canada (Commission on Fiscal Imbalance 2002; Lecours and Béland 2010).

A vigorous debate over the issue of fiscal imbalance emerged in the mid-1990s, when deficit elimination became a major priority of the federal government formed by the Liberal Party of Canada (LPC) after the 1993 elections. A crucial tool for reaching a balanced budget was a change in fiscal transfers to the provinces. In the 1960s and most of the 1970s, these transfers took the form of shared-cost programs: the federal government and the provinces would split costs for health care, higher education, and social assistance. In 1977, transfers for health care and higher education were changed to a block grant formula: the commitment of the federal government for helping to finance those fields was detached from provincial spending. However, the Canada Assistance Program (CAP), which ever since 1966 had transferred money to provinces to reimburse them for about half the costs incurred for social assistance and welfare, was left intact. With CAP, the federal government did not have full control over how much it was required to transfer to the provinces. In 1996, the federal government ended CAP as it consolidated its major vertical transfers into the Canada Health and Social Transfer (CHST), an omnibus block grant based on a formula independent of actual provincial spending on health care, education, and social assistance.

The Québec government, then formed by the Parti Québécois (PQ), criticized the changes harshly, as did other provinces. In the aftermath of the 1995 referendum on Québec sovereignty, the PQ denounced the federal government for balancing its budget "on the back of Quebeckers." It argued that the needy and the sick in the province were cared for by a Québec government that did not have the necessary resources to provide the best services possible, while the federal government's financial resources exceeded the needs associated with its constitutional responsibilities. The PQ labelled this situation "fiscal imbalance," and Québec's other political parties agreed. The Québec government created a commission (the Commission on Fiscal Imbalance) to study this problem and find a solution. In part to suggest the commission reflected a partisan consensus about the issue, the PQ named a former Liberal minister, Yves Séguin, as chair. In 2003, the Québec Liberal Party (QLP) formed the government in Québec and kept up the pressure on the Liberal Party of Canada to address the issue of fiscal imbalance. The QLP did not have to work hard to convince most other provincial governments that there was indeed a fiscal imbalance in the Canadian federation. Sensitive to the electoral implications of denying the notion of fiscal imbalance, all federal opposition parties acknowledged fiscal imbalance and promised to address it, if and when they took power.

The Conservative government formed after the 2006 elections produced a budget that gave considerable importance to the theme of fiscal imbalance. The new government argued for a different approach to federalism, labelled "open federalism," one that respected provincial jurisdictions and therefore refrained from creating new national programs. Although this approach followed none of the key recommendations of Québec's Commission on Fiscal Imbalance, which advocated most importantly for giving provinces a greater share of the "fiscal space" (primarily the sales tax) so they could augment their fiscal resources without raising income tax, the federal government declared that fiscal imbalance had been adequately addressed.[4] Québec and most of the other provinces did not accept this verdict; yet fiscal imbalance as a burning political issue disappeared from the federal policy agenda, perhaps in part because existing federal surpluses rapidly disappeared during the early Harper years.

The second type of fiscal gap featured in Canadian political and policy debates is horizontal, referring to "the differential capacities of the provinces to raise revenues" (Atkinson et al. 2013, 62). This form of fiscal gap points to enduring fiscal inequalities between constituent units, which reflect broader economic and territorial disparities. In Canada, alongside other factors such as patterns of industrialization, main reasons for these disparities include the provincial ownership and uneven geographic distribution of natural resources. Most provinces have natural resources of some

---

4 However, the Harper government enacted a two-point reduction in the federal GST (Goods and Services Tax), which gave provinces more room to raise their own PST (Provincial Sales Tax).

type: oil, gas, hydro-electricity, forestry, fisheries, and minerals. Not only are these resources unevenly spread out across the country but their value is also quite uneven: oil, especially when world prices are high, provides very important revenues. These revenues (whether they come from oil or other natural resources) go directly to the provincial government on whose territory the resources lie. The constitutional basis for the provincial ownership of natural resources is article 109 of the 1867 British North America Act: "All Lands, Mines, Minerals, and Royalties belonging to the several Provinces of Canada, Nova Scotia, and New Brunswick at the Union, and all Sums then due or payable for such Lands, Mines, Minerals, or Royalties, shall belong to the several Provinces of Ontario, Quebec, Nova Scotia, and New Brunswick." After the Trudeau government embarked on an oil price regulation policy in the early 1980s (more on the National Energy Program in the next chapter), provincial governments insisted that there be a "resource amendment" included in the 1982 constitutional reform. As a result, article 92 A states that "In each province, the legislature may exclusively make laws in relation to (a) exploration for non-renewable natural resources in the province; (b) development, conservation and management of non-renewable natural resources and forestry resources in the province; and (c) development, conservation and management of sites and facilities in the province for the generation and production of electrical energy." This amendment to the constitutional division of powers enhanced the legislative powers of the provinces (Moull 1987, 413).

The fact that provincial governments receive revenues stemming from resource exploitation taking place on their territory greatly impacts each province's fiscal capacity. Fiscal capacity refers to the ability of provinces "to raise revenue from their own sources" (Barro 2002, 1). In Canada, as in other federations, fiscal revenues raised by each constituent unit vary across jurisdictions and fluctuate over time. From a normative and a public policy standpoint, these differences are problematic because they can compromise the ability of poorer constituent units to deliver services of comparable quality to those delivered by their wealthier counterparts, without imposing an undue fiscal burden on their residents.

From a public policy standpoint, important discrepancies in provincial fiscal capacities could lead to out-migration from poorer provinces, so wealthier provinces would experience net in-migration. Arguably, the traditionally poorer provinces of the federation (Newfoundland, Prince Edward Island, New Brunswick, Nova Scotia, Manitoba, and Saskatchewan) could have lost even more population than they have lost had no equalization program been created (in all likelihood, Québec would not have suffered a similar fate since it would have been inherently difficult for its French-speaking majority, many of whom are unilingual, to migrate to an English-speaking labour market). The public policy problem of the economic development of poorer provinces would have been compounded by this loss in population. In turn, the institutional basis of the Canadian federation could have been destabilized insofar as important provincial population losses and gains would have called into question the delicate balance of provincial representation in the House of Commons.

From a normative perspective, important differences in the fiscal capacity of provinces challenge the meaning of Canadian citizenship, solidarity, and even nationhood. The development of the welfare state in Canada compensated for socio-economic inequalities (between individuals or social classes), but in the context of federalism, because provinces have an important role to play in social and education policy, there are limits on the capacity of the federal government to provide substance to the idea of Canadian social citizenship. Differences in means among provincial governments to offer social protection to their residents can present a serious challenge to the very notion of solidarity and, sometimes, of nationhood. Indeed, chronic and unmitigated territorial discrepancies may provide material for politicians to generate, build, or sustain feelings of resentment toward and alienation from the central state. In turn, those sentiments can compromise nationhood or exacerbate already existing phenomena of distinct "national" belongings associated with regions or provinces.

The primary goal of equalization programs in federations is therefore to reduce the horizontal fiscal gap among constituent units, so they have a similar capacity to provide roughly comparable public services at a similar rate of taxation. Equalization programs typically do not have strings attached so as to preserve the autonomy of these constituent units, which in turn can help keep centralization at bay. In other words, equalization programs seek to achieve horizontal fiscal redistribution while enhancing or at least preserving the political autonomy of constituent units (Théret 1999).

Most advanced industrialized federations operate standalone equalization programs. One significant exception is the United States.[5] From 1972 to 1986, the federal government ran a "revenue sharing" program that

---

5 In comparative policy and social science research, it has long been common to compare Canada to the United States (Leman 1977; Lipset 1990; Maioni 1998; Zuberi 2006). This comparison is particularly the case in the field of federalism studies, where it is both common and fruitful (Boushey and Luedtke 2006; Simeon 1995; Théret 1999; Watts 1987). That said, the absence of an equalization program in the United States obviously reduces the value of the comparative perspective with regard to the management of the horizontal fiscal gap.

featured equalization components but focused primarily on addressing the vertical fiscal imbalance between the federal government and both states and municipalities (Wallin 1998). The absence of a standalone equalization program in the United States is the product of three distinct factors: the lack of a direct threat to national unity after 1865, a limited emphasis on equal access to services associated with the notion of social citizenship, and the nature of American political institutions, particularly the power of the second chamber (the United States Senate), which would make the adoption of an equalization program unlikely even if some constituencies within the country supported the idea (Béland and Lecours 2014a).

Equalization programs can take many different forms. Designing and reforming such a program involves making choices about at least six different features. The first choice is the source of financing for the program. In Canada, equalization is financed from the general revenues of the federal government. Other federations have made different choices. For instance, in Australia, equalization payments to the six states and two territories come from the Goods and Services Tax (GST) the Commonwealth government has levied since 2000. Similarly, in Germany, part of the value-added tax (VAT) is allocated to the 16 states (*Länder*). In Brazil, equalization to states and municipalities comes from the sharing of revenues "from three main federal taxes: personal income taxes, corporate income taxes, and the elective VAT" (Watts 2008, 111). These examples illustrate the diversity of equalization financing across federal countries.

The second choice to be made concerns the degree of equalization to be achieved. In Canada, the operative words are "reasonably comparable," in relation to levels of public services, as per article 36(2) of the 1982 Constitution Act. In contrast, in Australia, the Commonwealth Grants Commission (CGC) has suggested that "State governments should receive funding from the Commonwealth such that, if each made the same effort to raise revenue from its own sources and operated at the same level of efficiency, each would have the capacity to provide services at the *same* standard" (CGC 2008, 27, emphasis added). In Germany, a 1999 judgement by the Federal Constitutional Court following a challenge of the federal equalization law by some of the "donor" *Länder* stated that the purpose of equalization in that country was to "diminish but not level" territorial disparities (Hueglin and Fenna 2015, 191).

The third choice is the structure of the transfers. In Canada, as in most other federal countries, equalization payments are made by the federal government. In Germany, however, they take the form of "direct horizontal transfers from the rich to the poor *Länder*," although the federal government provides "a final topping up through vertical supplementary transfers"

(Hueglin and Fenna 2015, 190). Interestingly, in Canadian political and media discourse, equalization is sometimes depicted as if the program entailed a direct flow of money from wealthier to poorer provinces, even though this has never been the case in reality (Lecours and Béland 2010). Moving toward such a system in Canada could prove extremely controversial, especially in resource-rich provinces such as Alberta.

The fourth choice involved in the design or reform of an equalization program is whether to equalize strictly on fiscal capacity or to also consider needs, that is, the cost of providing public services for specific constituent units of a federation. Indeed, constituent units with the same fiscal capacity may face greater costs in providing the exact same public service because of particular challenges. Sometimes, the challenges can be related to demography. For example, offering long-term care to the elderly in a province with a higher percentage of older people would be especially expensive. At other times, it can be linked to geography. For example, delivering public services to people living in remote areas typically generates higher costs than delivering them to people living in a geographical area with a highly concentrated population. There is often some tension between those who prefer a strictly equalizing fiscal capacity—a simpler approach—and those who feel that a needs-based approach is more equitable even if more complex.

The fifth choice concerns the governance structure for equalization. The primary issue here is who will have decision-making power over the equalization formula used to calculate payments. In other words, what public authority decides which constituent units receive equalization money and how much. The broad parameters of equalization, for example if needs are considered as well as fiscal capacity, can also be influenced by the source of authority behind the program. In Canada, the federal government is the only formal decision maker for the program. Provinces are often consulted, but there is no obligation on the part of the federal government to consider their position, if there are consultations at all. In Australia, an arm's-length commission, the CGC, makes an annual recommendation for the "relativities" to be paid to the states. These "relativities" determine the share of the GST that goes to each state, inclusive of an equalization component. The Commonwealth government is under no obligation to follow the recommendation of the CGC, but the arm's-length agency has a reputation for technocratic expertise and neutrality that gives great credibility to its recommendation.

The sixth choice to make when designing or reforming an equalization program is determining its formal legal foundation. Canada constitutionalized the commitment of the federal government to make equalization payments. Germany also constitutionalized equalization. Article 107 (2) of the Basic Law of the Federal Republic of Germany speaks of the "reasonable equalisation of the disparate financial capacities of the *Länder*." In Australia, by contrast, equalization is not constitutionalized.

We will now focus on the historical development of the equalization program in Canada. In telling this story, we highlight the context in which some of the choices related to the design of equalization programs were made.

The historical development of equalization policy in Canada

Rowell-Sirois, the Québec question, and the birth of equalization

Although equalization only emerged as a stand-alone federal program in Canada in 1957, horizontal fiscal redistribution existed long before that (Courchene 1984, 65; Stevenson 2007, 3). In fact, provincial financial redistribution is as old as the 1867 British North America (BNA) Act. As economist Tom Courchene (1984) reminds us, the BNA Act featured statutory federal subsidies to the provinces that "contained an element of equalization in that they were per capita grants up to a maximum population" (65). Yet, importantly, the idea of a formal equalization program only moved into the federal policy arena in the late 1930s. At the time, the Great Depression and, more specifically, the fiscal crisis it created called into question existing federal-provincial arrangements. This was because "the mismatch between taxation powers and constitutional responsibilities had by the 1930s clearly reached unacceptable proportions" (Milne 1998, 181).

Set up in 1937 and reporting in 1940, the Rowell-Sirois Commission (Royal Commission on Dominion-Provincial Relations), tasked to assess provincial-federal relations in a changing economic context, spent much time studying the issue of horizontal fiscal redistribution, both in Canada and abroad. Its report formulated a coherent but controversial solution to the growing mismatch between taxation powers and constitutional responsibilities in Canada (Royal Commission on Dominion-Provincial Relations 1940, vol. 2). The Rowell-Sirois Report adopted a more centralizing perspective as it advocated the creation of purely federal social programs, such as unemployment insurance, as well as a sweeping concentration of fiscal powers in the hands of the federal government (for a critical discussion of the report's perceived centralizing bias, see Ferguson and Wardhaugh 2003). On the one hand, the Rowell-Sirois Commission recommended a permanent centralization of personal and income taxes as well as succession duties, a situation that would have increased the fiscal power of the federal government. On the other hand, to reduce fiscal inequalities among provinces, the commission also suggested the creation of National Adjustment Grants tasked with transferring money to the provinces on the basis of fiscal needs (Courchene 1984, 65). For the commission, these grants would have the double advantage of preserving provincial autonomy and fostering national unity by making sure the inhabitants of poorer provinces did not feel they had been left behind (Royal Commission on Dominion-Provincial Relations 1940, 2: 79).

The Rowell-Sirois Report proposed an equalization system for Canada that made two specific recommendations with respect to design (Béland and Lecours 2011). First, while taking into consideration the provinces' fiscal capacity, the proposed system would also evaluate their particular expenditure needs. Thus, in contrast to the system eventually adopted in 1957 and much like the Australian model, "the adjustment grants would have had both a revenue and an expenditure component" (Brown 1996, 13). Second, a financial commission similar to Australia's Commonwealth Grants Commission would advise Ottawa on the allocation of the National Adjustment Grants (Royal Commission on Dominion-Provincial Relations 1940, 2: 86).

In its chapter on the proposed National Adjustment Grants, the Rowell-Sirois Report did not refer to the Australian model. Yet, there is evidence that the inspiration for the proposed scheme came from that country. For instance, the commissioners consulted directly with Australian scholar and civil servant Lyndhurst Falkiner Giblin, who had played a major role in setting up his country's Commonwealth Grants Commission back in 1933 (Bird 1986, 141). Five years later, in August 1938, Giblin himself appeared before the Rowell-Sirois Commission (Royal Commission on Dominion-Provincial Relations 1940, 2: 216).

Despite the fact that the equalization system created in 1957 would profoundly differ from the approach formulated more than 15 years earlier by the Rowell-Sirois Commission, the commission's report offered a clear and lasting rationale for the adoption of a federal equalization program in Canada: "*each level of government in our federation should have the requisite financial means and financial security to carry out its constitutional responsibilities*" (Milne 1998, 181, emphasis in the original).

In the 1950s, the decline of the tax rental agreements between Ottawa and the provinces provided the immediate stimulus for the modern equalization policy in Canada (Courchene 1984, 27–35). Established in 1941 to finance the war effort, these centralizing yet temporary agreements stipulated that "the provinces agreed to vacate the income tax and estate tax fields in return for 'rental' payments" from the federal government

(Sheikh and Carreau 2000, 14). Importantly, such agreements "took into account differences in fiscal capacity through per capita payments (implicit equalization) and provided minimum base grants to poorer provinces" (Marchildon 2005, 422). Soon after the end of World War II, a series of developments in Québec, then controlled by the conservative nationalist and autonomist Union Nationale government of Maurice Duplessis, gradually weakened the tax rental system adopted during the war. For instance, though "Quebec signed the 1941 rental agreement, it refused to be party to the others (1946, 1952 and 1957).... In 1947, Quebec introduced its own corporate income tax" (Madore 1997, 3). More important, in 1954, the Duplessis government decided to reimpose the Québec income tax. As David Milne (1998) states, this decision, and the publication in 1956 of Québec's autonomist *Tremblay Report*, made it clear that "any trade off of equalization for federal occupation of the central tax sources ... was impossible" (190). In the wake of Québec's decision on its income tax, moreover, "providing equalization payments, regardless of whether or not a particular province rented its tax fields to the national government, would be a way of ending the isolation of Quebec" (Bryden 2009, 81). Thus, the creation in 1957 of the federal equalization program can be understood in part as an attempt to break the recent fiscal and institutional isolation of Québec within the Canadian federal system (Pickersgill 1975, 309). In Canada, equalization played a role in accommodating sub-state nationalism in the politically contentious context of a divided, multinational state (Béland and Lecours 2014b).

As created, the 1957 equalization program did share some features with the model outlined in the 1940 Rowell-Sirois Report. For instance, as Courchene (1984) wrote, "the fact that equalization payments are transferred unconditionally to the recipient provinces probably owes a great deal to the Rowell-Sirois Commission's emphasis on fiscal autonomy" (39). Yet Courchene (1984) also reminds us that it would be a mistake to think that the new program was simply "a natural outgrowth of the Commission's arguments for National Adjustments Grants" (38). In fact, the 1957 program differed from the National Adjustment Grants advocated in the 1940 Rowell-Sirois Report in at least two major ways. First, Ottawa rejected their needs-based approach and, instead, created a program focused exclusively on the assessment of the provinces' fiscal capacity. Thus, starting in 1957, "Provinces would receive a grant if the revenue they could generate from three taxes at a given tax rate was less than what the two richest provinces of the day could generate at those same rates" (Marchildon 2005, 422). Second, instead of setting up an arm's-length expert body similar to Australia's Commonwealth Grants

Commission, the federal government managed the equalization system and determined the entitlements for provinces falling below the average fiscal capacity (MacNevin 2004, 188). To account for these two choices, we need to go back to the criticisms formulated by the provinces against the Rowell-Sirois approach to equalization while at the same time understanding these grievances in the context of the enduring idea of provincial autonomy (Béland and Lecours 2011).

For the Rowell-Sirois Commission, the creation of a federal equalization program, combined with permanent fiscal centralization, represented a solution to both the horizontal and vertical fiscal gaps present in the 1930s. Yet, in the name of provincial autonomy, some provinces opposed the commission's report and the permanent fiscal centralization it advocated. For example, at a 1941 dominion-provincial conference, Ontario, heavily supported by Québec, led the opposition against the commission's recommendations (Bryden 2009, 77). Because of the opposition of Canada's most populous and powerful provinces, the conference "turned out to be a fiasco" and the Rowell-Sirois recommendations on equalization and permanent fiscal centralization were not implemented (Betcherman 2002, 329).

After the war, Québec and the Union Nationale government of Premier Maurice Duplessis were the strongest advocates for provincial autonomy. The Duplessis government constantly attacked perceived federal intrusions into provincial matters. For instance, when Ottawa adopted a national family allowance scheme in 1944, Premier Duplessis denounced it as a direct attack against both provincial autonomy and French-Canadian families.[6] As indicated previously, in the name of provincial autonomy, the Duplessis government became the first province to exit the tax rental system created during the war (Courchene 1984). This move contributed to the need for Ottawa to implement an equalization program that would reduce the isolation of Québec by maintaining some form of territorial redistribution outside the tax rental system without threatening the provincial autonomy Duplessis defended so aggressively (Béland and Lecours 2014b; Bryden 2009). Because Duplessis would have depicted Ottawa assessing expenditure needs as an intrusion into provincial matters, the idea of a needs-based equalization formula was rejected, a casualty of the growing intergovernmental tensions between Québec and the federal government (Pickersgill 1975, 106).

---

6 At first, the program penalized large families, which were overrepresented in Québec's Catholic society (Marshall 1994).

Ontario also played a key role in discussions leading up to the adoption of the federal equalization program in 1957. Ontario was the wealthiest province in the country at the time, and its government recognized that, in the context of its fiscal negotiations with Ottawa that emphasized strengthening provincial taxation rights, backing the idea of a new equalization program would help generate the support Ontario needed from poorer provinces, such as New Brunswick, for more provincial autonomy in the realm of taxation (Bryden 2009). Like Québec, Ontario had long supported the idea of provincial autonomy. To this end, Ontario worked closely with Québec to oppose federal proposals they both considered to be overly centralizing (Cameron and Simeon 1997, 163).

After 1945, although Ontario and Québec officials frequently disagreed on basic policy choices, their bold defence of provincial autonomy transformed them into "strange bedfellows" in the context of key political fights with Ottawa (Bryden 2000, 385). For instance, in the context of the 1945–46 Dominion-Provincial Reconstruction Conference, Ontario Premier George Drew worked closely with Premier Duplessis to oppose federal plans to further centralize Canada's fiscal arrangements. The alliance between the two largest provinces of the country, known as the "Drew-Duplessis axis," challenged centralization in the name of provincial autonomy (Bryden 2000, 386). In light of this post-1945 rejection of fiscal centralism and the promotion of provincial autonomy by these two politically powerful provinces, it is hardly surprising that the equalization program adopted in 1957 differed so much from the one formulated in the widely criticized Rowell-Sirois Report (Brown 1996, 23). Indeed, the model proposed in the 1940 Rowell-Sirois Report would have been perceived by these two provinces as an intolerable federal intrusion in provincial matters. As Milne (1998) states,

> The decision to proceed with a system of revenue equalization
> based in a representative tax-system approach rather than
> one addressed to expenditure needs also owed a good deal to
> the growing political power of provincialism in Quebec and
> elsewhere. In this climate, the adoption of the Australian model
> of equalization was clearly regarded as so intrusive as to be
> unworkable. (191)[7]

---

7 For a similar perspective, see Leslie (1988, 28).

The staunch defence of provincial autonomy by the most powerful premiers in the country may help account for Ottawa's 1957 decision to have the federal government, rather than an arm's-length body, assess the fiscal capacity of the provinces, as well as for the decision to reject an evaluation of expenditure needs. In the end, the approach adopted in 1957 received general support from the provinces. Provinces did not challenge the source of financing (it was always assumed the program would be run by the federal government and financed from its general revenues) or the structure of transfers (a direct province-to-province transfer was unthinkable in the context of the provincial defence of autonomy). Provinces also never pushed for the creation of an Australian-style, arm's-length commission or for the inclusion of service needs in the equalization formula (Béland and Lecours 2014b). In the absence of any comprehensive constitutional talks at that time, there was no serious suggestion that equalization be enshrined in the Canadian Constitution, nor was there any principled statement about the desired comprehensiveness of equalization.

The evolution of equalization

From its creation in 1957 to the early 2000s, the equalization program witnessed many incremental changes that were primarily technical and did not alter the basic structure of equalization policy in Canada.[8] Such changes to the equalization formula (see text box) typically took place every five years, when the time came to review the program.

One key area of change to the program concerned the type of tax revenues included in the federal equalization formula. Originally, the formula only considered three provincial sources of revenue: income taxes, corporate taxes, and succession duties. In 1957, these were the only well-documented taxes present in all of the 10 provinces, which is why the federal government limited the formula to these three taxes. In 1967, the formula had grown to include no fewer than 16 provincial revenue sources. In addition to the three original revenue sources, the extended list included sales tax, motor fuel tax, alcoholic beverage revenues, forestry revenues, and oil royalties (Perry 1997, 128). Over time, the number of provincial revenue sources used in the equalization formula further increased, reaching 27 by the late 1970s (MacNevin 2004, 193) and 33 in the 1980s. This

---

8 The following historical discussion draws on Lecours and Béland (2010).

The Equalization Formula

Primary variations in the equalization formula over time are due to changes in three factors. The first is the "standard" that is used as a reference point in determining the target per capita revenues. The second relates to the categories of revenues that are included in the calculation. The third consideration is whether actual revenues or representative revenues (based on average tax rates) are used in the assessment of revenues. Once these decisions are made, the formula that determines province p's equalization entitlement is some version of this:

$$standard\ per\ capita\ fiscal\ capacity -$$
$$province\ p's\ fiscal\ capacity = entitlement\ of\ p.$$

Practical considerations have often been the overriding determinant of the choices that dictate how the standard is defined, the revenue types that are included and excluded, and the use of actual versus representative revenues. These practical considerations usually relate to what is manageable from the federal government's point of view given its budget constraints.

staggering multiplication of the tax sources taken into consideration by the equalization formula increased its complexity over time.[9]

Of course, increasing the number of tax sources used in the formula had consequences for the provinces, and, in the first decades of equalization, the federal government typically met with them to hear their position on a proposal for change and attempted to address their concerns. For example, the provinces used a meeting of the Federal-Provincial Tax Structure Committee to present their views on the 1966–67 proposed reform that added a dozen new taxes to the formula. Several provinces opposed the reform, including Saskatchewan, because it would see its equalization payments drop. Prince Edward Island objected because it did not want the expansion of the program to come at the expense of grants designed to support the Atlantic provinces. In the end, the federal government established a transition period

---

9 Interestingly, in 1967, when a major increase in the number of revenue sources used in the equalization formula took place, the federal government borrowed the "representative tax system" (RTS)—now used to calculate provincial fiscal capacity—from a foreign expert panel, namely the US Advisory Commission on Intergovernmental Relations, which had put forward this model five years earlier (Bird and Slack 1990, 916).

and "stabilization provisions" for Saskatchewan and similar protection commitments for the Atlantic provinces (Perry 1997, 128).

An enduring source of policy change over time for the equalization
program is the number of provinces used to determine an equalization standard. For instance, in 1962, a decision was made that "equalization would
now be based on the average per capita revenue of all ten provinces rather
than on the average for the two most revenue-rich provinces" (Perry 1997,
120). As this change disadvantaged the four Atlantic provinces; Ottawa
raised the special adjustment grants that had been created for them half a
decade earlier (Perry 1997, 120). The new 10-province standard survived
until 1982, when the federal government adopted a five-province standard, which was designed to exclude both the richest (Alberta) and the
four poorest provinces (New Brunswick, Newfoundland, Nova Scotia, and
Prince Edward Island) from the calculation of average fiscal capacity. The
logic underlying this change was to control the cost of the program for the
federal budget by excluding Alberta's large oil revenues from the determination of the equalization standard.

The adoption in 1982 of a five-province standard points to the growing
role over time of revenues from non-renewable resources such as oil and
natural gas in Canadian equalization policy. In 1962, the federal government started to take into account 50 per cent of provincial natural resource
revenues in its assessment of provincial fiscal capacity. Even if Alberta
would receive equalization payments for several more years under a special
guarantee provision, this federal decision altered the status of Alberta from
a receiving to a non-receiving province, a status that it has retained ever
since (Courchene 1984, 42–43; Lecours and Béland 2010).

Rapid increases in oil revenues after the 1973 energy crisis created a
strong fiscal challenge to the federal equalization system (Perry 1997). To
address the impact of high energy prices and tax revenues on equalization,
the federal government adopted emergency measures (MacNevin 2004,
193). For instance, the 1974 budget introduced a seemingly arbitrary distinction in the equalization formula between "basic revenues" and "additional revenues" (from oil and gas) as a result of the rapid and unexpected
price increases stemming directly from the 1973 energy crisis (Perry 1997,
134–35). In the late 1970s, growing resource revenues meant that Ontario,
the most populous province by far, would qualify for equalization payments,
something the federal government as well as the provinces, including
Ontario, found intolerable (Perry 1997, 140). To avoid this scenario, the
new federal law excluded "from equalization payments any province with
per capita personal income that was regularly above the national average"
(Perry 1997, 140). In the end, Ontario did not receive federal equalization

payments, and, in 1982, the adoption of the five-province standard became a more permanent solution to the energy resource problem (Lecours and Béland 2010).

The early 1980s witnessed a period of intense constitutional negotiation. Prime Minister Pierre Trudeau was determined to patriate the Canadian Constitution from the United Kingdom and to place in the Constitution a Charter of Rights and Freedoms. In the context of such an agenda for constitutional change, many other items crept onto the agenda, including equalization. Once the window was opened, there seemed to be a general consensus to go ahead and constitutionalize the principle of equalization payments. Indeed, the negotiations leading to the 1982 Constitution Act were very acrimonious about the Charter, among other things, but not about equalization. In the end, article 36(2) of the Constitution Act states that "Parliament and the government of Canada are committed to the principle of making equalization payments to ensure that provincial governments have sufficient revenues to provide reasonably comparable levels of public services at reasonably comparable levels of taxation."

This article provides a statement of principle about the aim and scope of equalization: *comparable* levels of public services are the objective, not the *same* levels. This policy was consistent with the political discourse in the country about what the equalization program should achieve. For example, in a 1966 statement, then Finance Minister Mitchell Sharp used the term "adequate" when characterizing the level of public services that should be attained in each province. The constitutionalization of equalization also provides some protection for provinces against a federal government that might wish to terminate the program. However, this protection may not be as strong as it appears, in part because what is constitutionalized is the federal government's commitment to the *principle* of making equalization payments. As a consequence, there is really nothing about the specific workings of equalization that could be enforceable in court (Kellock and LeRoy 2007, 27–29).

At the same time, because equalization payments are completely unconditional, a province is in fact not obliged to provide public services comparable to those available in other provinces, despite the spirit of article 36 (2). Hence, what equalization does is simply offer less well-off provinces a more realistic possibility of being able to offer such comparable services than if they did not receive equalization payments.

In the late 1980s, provinces sought to take advantage of another round of broad constitutional negotiations launched by Progressive Conservative Prime Minister Brian Mulroney to tighten the language of the equalization article. After the failure of the Meech Lake Accord that sought to gain the signature of Québec's government to the amended Canadian Constitution (Québec had not signed the 1982 Constitution Act), another attempt was made at a constitutional agreement that would not only satisfy Québec's demands but also address the concerns of other provinces and of Indigenous peoples. In this context, provinces saw an opportunity to strengthen the standing of equalization in the Constitution. They successfully proposed to insert the following clause in the Charlottetown Accord: "Parliament and the Government of Canada are committed to making equalization payments so that provincial governments have sufficient revenues to provide *reasonably comparable* levels of public services at *reasonably comparable* levels of taxation" (emphasis added). With this phrasing, the federal government would be committed not merely to the principle of equalization but to making payments to the provinces. The Charlottetown Accord also stipulated that the "Constitution should commit the federal government to meaningful consultation with the provinces before introducing legislation relating to equalization payments." Because the accord was never implemented (it failed to gain majority support in all provinces and in the country as a whole in an October 1992 referendum), the only constitutional specification of equalization remains article 36 of the 1982 Constitution Act.

In the early to mid-1990s, large budget deficits meant that fiscal austerity dominated the policy agenda. The Liberal government of Jean Chrétien enacted cuts to both federal social programs and transfers to the provinces in an attempt to balance the federal budget. For example, announced as part of the austerity-laden and controversial 1995 federal budget, the Canada Health and Social Transfer deeply and suddenly cut federal transfers for health care, social assistance, and postsecondary education (Banting 2005; Bashevkin 2000). In that period, fiscal austerity impacted the federal equalization program through the imposition of a cap on total equalization payments "to a rate of growth no higher than that of the gross national product" (Perry 1997, 162). In stark contrast to federal social transfers, however, equalization never faced direct, explicit, and politically controversial cutbacks. As David Milne (1998) states, "no other fiscal program has … been so insulated from the savage series of federal restraint measures in the 1990s" (193). A possible explanation for that is that ad hoc adjustments, for example the equalization cap and the shift to the five-province standard in 1982, helped limit the overall fiscal weight of the program over time. In fact, as "a share of total federal revenue, [equalization fell] from a high of almost 7.8 per cent in 1984 to a low of roughly 5.6 per cent in 2001" (Marchildon 2005, 422). Another potential explanation for the absence of direct cuts to equalization payments is that they would have affected only less well-off provinces, but cuts to health and social transfers affected all the provinces, thus potentially reducing political costs for Ottawa.

Direct cuts in equalization payments therefore proved unnecessary during the austerity of the mid-to late 1990s, as the relative fiscal weight of the program had declined. Even during this period, although economists and policy experts such as Dan Usher (1995) criticized the federal equalization program and called for bold change, the political consensus surrounding equalization remained strong within the federal political arena. With the partial exception of the Reform Party, which called for a more targeted federal program (Milne 1998, 199), all the federal parties supported equalization, possibly in part because of the electoral weight of receiving provinces (Lecours and Béland 2010).

Explaining fundamental equalization choices: A comparative perspective with Australia

The creation of a stand-alone equalization program in 1957 represented a milestone for Canadian political development, not only because it established mechanisms to reduce the consequences of territorial disparities but also because it embedded equalization in broader notions of Canadian citizenship, solidarity, and nationhood. Provinces that are typically equalization recipients consider equalization payments a "right" of Canadian citizenship and an expression of Canadian solidarity and of Canadian national unity. Although conflict around equalization erupts from time to time (as will be seen in the next chapter), even traditionally non-recipient provinces view equalization largely as a positive contributor to the Canadian political community (Alberta being a partial exception).

If we are to gain greater insight into the development of equalization in Canada, it is useful to have a comparative perspective. For this, we turn to Australia, another federation frequently compared to Canada (Béland and Lecours 2011; Coleman and Skogstad 1995; Hodgins et al. 1989; Obinger, Leibfried, and Castles 2005). Beyond the key historical and institutional similarities between these two Commonwealth countries, similarities stemming in part from their colonial past, it is appropriate to turn to Australia because it created the first system of equalization in the 1930s. Also, as we discussed previously, the Australian model served as a reference point for Canadian policy specialists in the late 1930s and early 1940s when the idea of instituting an equalization system made its way into federal policy debates.

First of all, there are some parallels between the birth of equalization programs in Canada and Australia. The story of the development of equalization in Australia validates some of the points already made about the impulse behind the establishment of the Canadian equalization program in 1957. Australia, like Canada, is a large federation with a stand-alone equalization system created partly to mitigate territorial conflict. The creation of the CGC in 1933, which formalized Australia's equalization system, was prompted in part by a secessionist movement in Western Australia, whose grievances were primarily of an economic nature. Western Australia even held a referendum in which a majority voted for independence. Although Australia is now widely considered to be a territorially homogenous country (Fenna 2007), it was not always, and secessionism in Western Australia provided an incentive for creating an equalization system in that country just as national unity concerns linked to Québec favoured the creation of Canadian equalization.

When the time came to design and implement an equalization system in 1957, Canadian decision makers made some different policy choices than their Australian counterparts. Most important, Canada chose to base its equalization formula strictly on fiscal capacity (the revenue side) rather than also considering needs (the cost side). Furthermore, Canada favoured federal executive discretion in the management of the program rather than using an arm's-length agency.

Why did Canadian federal and provincial officials not favour incorporating a needs component into the equalization formula? To answer this question requires a broad understanding of federalism in Canada and Australia. Australian federalism has had a clear centralizing trajectory (Fenna 2007). The Commonwealth government is incontestably the most important government in the eyes of Australians, and its strong presence in a multiplicity of policy fields is not only tolerated but desired. In Canada, the historical trajectory of federalism is quite different. Created as a centralized federation, the evolution has been toward a gradual empowerment of the provinces, which have defined political communities with strong identities. Hence, Canadian provinces strongly value their autonomy, are usually ready to defend it, and can count on their residents for support.

The consequence of these differences in the federal dynamics of Canada and Australia for the design of equalization systems is that, in Australia, the assessment of expenditure needs was widely accepted as legitimate, whereas, in Canada, it was considered an outright intrusion into provincial affairs. In fact, in Canada, in the rare instances when this option was raised, provincial autonomy moved to the forefront of the debate and became a direct obstacle to its adoption (Leslie 1988, 28; McLarty 1997, 207). Knowing that introducing needs assessment would be perceived as an intrusive move by at least some provinces (given the on-site scrutiny that is implied), federal officials have seldom been keen to promote this controversial policy option (Béland and Lecours 2011).

The decision not to create an arm's-length body similar to Australia's Commonwealth Grants Commission to manage equalization in Canada also can be linked to the distinct natures of Australian and Canadian federalism. The strength of Canadian provinces has meant that they see themselves as equal partners with the federal government in the management of the federation; they have therefore been loath to endorse a governance structure in which an arm's-length agency would potentially limit the agency of provinces in shaping decision making on equalization. Of course, provincial governments play no formal role in the management of equalization, and the federal government does not even have a formal obligation to consult them, even on important decisions. However, the existence of dense networks of intergovernmental relations means that provinces can potentially reach, and indeed exercise, some leverage on the federal government when it comes to equalization.

Conclusion

Both change and continuity have characterized equalization in Canada since its creation in 1957. The governing structure of the program based on federal executive discretion and its basic logic of using fiscal capacity to determine payments to provinces have remained unchanged. This being said, many changes have been made to the program over the years, whether these are related to the number of provinces used to determine the equalization standard or to how non-renewable natural resource revenues are factored into the formula. In some instances, reforms (or reform proposals) generated heated political debate. Indeed, there is an inherent potential for the politicization of equalization within Canadian federalism, which means that the program can become the subject of intergovernmental conflict. We develop this idea further in the next chapter as we focus more clearly on the politics of equalization in Canada.

References

Atkinson, Michael M., Daniel Béland, Gregory P. Marchildon, Kathleen McNutt, Peter W.B. Phillips, and Ken Rasmussen. 2013. *Governance and Public Policy in Canada: A View from the Provinces*. Toronto: University of Toronto Press.

Banting, Keith. 2005. "Canada: Nation-Building in a Federal Welfare State." In *Federalism and the Welfare State: New World and European Experiences*, edited by Herbert Obinger, Stephan Leibfried, and Francis G. Castles, 89–137. Cambridge: Cambridge University Press. http://dx.doi.org/10.1017/CBO9780511491856.005.

Barro, Stephen M. 2002. *Macroeconomic versus RTS Measures of Fiscal Capacity: Theoretical Foundations and Implication for Canada*. Kingston, ON: Institute of Intergovernmental Relations.

Bashevkin, Sylvia. 2000. "Rethinking Retrenchment: North American Social Policy during the Early Clinton and Chrétien Years." *Canadian Journal of Political Science* 33 (1): 7–36. http://dx.doi.org/10.1017/S0008423900000020.

Béland, Daniel, and André Lecours. 2011. "The Ideational Dimension of Federalism: The 'Australian Model' and the Politics of Equalization in Canada." *Australian Journal of Political Science* 46 (2): 199–212. http://dx.doi.org/10.1080/10361146.2011.567974.

Béland, Daniel, and André Lecours. 2014a. "Fiscal Federalism and American Exceptionalism: Why Is There No Federal Equalisation System in the United States?" *Journal of Public Policy* 34 (2): 303–29. http://dx.doi.org/10.1017/S0143814X14000038.

Béland, Daniel, and André Lecours. 2014b. "Accommodation and the Politics of Fiscal Equalization in Multinational States: The Case of Canada." *Nations and Nationalism* 20 (2): 337–54. http://dx.doi.org/10.1111/nana.12049.

Béland, Daniel, and André Lecours. 2016. *Canada's Equalization Policy in Comparative Perspective*. IRPP Insight No. 9. Montréal: Institute for Research on Public Policy.

Betcherman, Lita-Rose. 2002. *Ernest Lapointe: Mackenzie King's Great Quebec Lieutenant*. Toronto: University of Toronto Press.

Bird, Richard M. 1986. *Federal Finance in Comparative Perspective*. Toronto: Canadian Tax Foundation.

Bird, Richard M., and Enid Slack. 1990. "Equalization: The Representative Tax System Revisited." *Canadian Tax Journal* 38 (4): 913–27.

Boushey, Graeme, and Adam Luedtke. 2006. "Fiscal Federalism and the Politics of Immigration: Centralized and Decentralized Immigration Policies in Canada and the United States." *Journal of Comparative Policy Analysis* 8 (3): 207–24. http://dx.doi.org/10.1080/13876980600858481.

Brown, Douglas M. 1996. *Equalization on the Basis of Need in Canada*. Reflections Paper No. 15. Kingston: Institute of Intergovernmental Relations.

Bryden, P.E. 2000. "The Ontario-Quebec Axis: Postwar Strategies in Intergovernmental Negotiations." In *Ontario since Confederation: A Reader*, edited by Edgar-André Montigny and Anne Lorene Chambers, 381–408. Toronto: University of Toronto Press.

Bryden, P.E. 2009. "The Obligations of Federalism: Ontario and the Origins of Equalization." In *Framing Canadian Federalism: Historical Essays in Honour of John T. Saywell*, edited by Dimitry Anastakis and Penny Bryden, 75–94. Toronto: University of Toronto Press. http://dx.doi.org/10.3138/9781442688131-005.

Cameron, David, and Richard Simeon. 1997. "Ontario in Confederation: The Not-So-Friendly Giant." In *The Government and Politics of Ontario*, edited by Graham White, 158–85. Toronto: University of Toronto Press.

CGC (Commonwealth Grants Commission). 2008. *The Commonwealth Grants Commission: The Last 25 Years*. Canberra: Commonwealth Grants Commission.

Coleman, William D., and Grace Skogstad. 1995. "Neo-liberalism, Policy Networks, and Policy Change: Agricultural Policy Reform in Australia and Canada." *Australian Journal of Political Science* 30 (2): 242–63. http://dx.doi.org/10.1080/00323269508402335.

Commission on Fiscal Imbalance. 2002. *A New Division of Canada's Financial Resources: Report*. Quebec City: Government of Québec. http://www.groupes.finances.gouv.qc.ca/desequilibrefiscal/en/pdf/rapport_final_en.pdf.

Courchene, Thomas J. 1984. *Equalization Payments: Past, Present, and Future*. Toronto: Ontario Economic Council.

Fenna, Alan. 2007. "The Malaise of Federalism: Comparative Reflections on Commonwealth-State Relations." *Australian Journal of Public Administration* 66 (3): 298–306. http://dx.doi.org/10.1111/j.1467-8500.2007.00551.x.

Ferguson, Barry, and Robert Wardhaugh. 2003. "'Impossible Conditions of Inequality': John W. Dafoe, the Rowell-Sirois Royal Commission, and the Interpretation of Canadian Federalism." *Canadian Historical Review* 84 (4): 551–84. http://dx.doi.org/10.3138/CHR.84.4.551.

Hodgins, Bruce W., John J. Eddy, Shelagh D. Grant, and James Struthers, eds. 1989. *Federalism in Canada and Australia: Historical Perspectives, 1920–1988*. Peterborough: Broadview Press.

Hueglin, Thomas O., and Alan Fenna. 2015. *Comparative Federalism: A Systematic Inquiry*. 2nd ed. Toronto: University of Toronto Press.

Kellock, Burton H., and Sylvia LeRoy. 2007. "Questioning the Legality of Equalization." In *Beyond Equalization: Examining Fiscal Transfers in a Broader Context*, edited by Jason Clemens and Niels Veldhuis, 25–45. Toronto: The Fraser Institute.

Lecours, André, and Daniel Béland. 2010. "Federalism and Fiscal Policy: The Politics of Equalization in Canada." *Publius: The Journal of Federalism* 40 (4): 569–96. http://dx.doi.org/10.1093/publius/pjp030.

Leman, Christopher. 1977. "Patterns of Policy Development: Social Security in the United States and Canada." *Public Policy* 25: 261–91.

Leslie, Peter M. 1988. *National Citizenship and Provincial Communities: A Review of Canadian Fiscal Federalism*. Kingston: Institute of Intergovernmental Relations.

Lipset, Seymour Martin. 1990. *Continental Divide: The Values and Institutions of the United States and Canada*. New York: Routledge.

MacNevin, Alex S. 2004. *The Canadian Federal-Provincial Equalization Regime: An Assessment*. Canadian Tax Paper No. 109. Toronto: Canadian Tax Foundation.

Madore, Odette. 1997. *The Transfer of Tax Points to Provinces under the Canada Health and Social Transfer*. Background Paper No. BP-450E. Ottawa: Parliamentary Research Branch. http://publications.gc.ca/collections/Collection-R/LoPBdP/BP-e/bp450-e.pdf.

Maioni, Antonia. 1998. *Parting at the Crossroads: The Emergence of Health Insurance in the United States and Canada*. Princeton: Princeton University Press.

Marchildon, Gregory P. 2005. "Understanding Equalization: Is It Possible?" *Canadian Public Administration* 48 (3): 420–28. http://dx.doi.org/10.1111/j.1754-7121.2005.tb00233.x.

Marshall, Dominique. 1994. "Nationalisme et politiques sociales au Québec depuis 1867: Un siècle de rendez-vous manqués entre l'État, l'Église et les familles." *British Journal of Canadian Studies* 9: 301–47.

McLarty, Robert A. 1997. "Econometric Analysis and Public Policy: The Case of Fiscal Need Assessment." *Canadian Public Policy* 23 (2): 203–8. http://dx.doi.org/10.2307/3551485.

Milne, David. 1998. "Equalization and the Politics of Restraint." In *Equalization: Its Contribution to Canada's Fiscal and Economic Progress*, edited by Robin W. Boadway and Paul A.R. Hobson, 175–204. Kingston, ON: John Deutsch Institute for the Study of Economic Policy, Queen's University.

Moull, William D. 1987. "Natural Resources and Canadian Federalism: Reflections on a Turbulent Decade." *Osgoode Hall Law Journal* 25 (2): 411–29.

Obinger, Herbert, Stephan Leibfried, and Francis G. Castles, eds. 2005. *Federalism and the Welfare State: New World and European Experiences*. Cambridge: Cambridge University Press. http://dx.doi.org/10.1017/CBO9780511491856.

Perry, David B. 1997. *Financing the Canadian Federation, 1867 to 1995: Setting the Stage for Change*. Toronto: Canadian Tax Foundation.

Pickersgill, J.W. 1975. *My Years with Louis St Laurent: A Political Memoir*. Toronto: University of Toronto Press.

Royal Commission on Dominion-Provincial Relations. 1940. *Report of the Royal Commission on Dominion-Provincial Relations*. 3 vols. Ottawa: King's Printer.

Sheikh, Munir A., and Michel Carreau. 2000. "A Federal Perspective on the Role and Operation of the Tax Collection Agreements." In *Federal Administration of Provincial Taxes: New Directions*, 9–28. Ottawa: Department of Finance. First published in 1999.

Simeon, Richard. 1995. "Canada and the United States: Lessons from the North American Experience." In *Rethinking Federalism: Citizens, Markets, and Governments in a Changing World*, edited by Karen Knop, Sylvia Ostry, Richard Simeon, and Katherine Swinton, 250–72. Vancouver: UBC Press.

Stevenson, Garth. 2007. "Fiscal Federalism and the Burden of History." Paper presented at Queen's Institute of Intergovernmental Relations' conference, Fiscal Federalism and the Future of Canada, Kingston, ON, 28–29 September 2006. In Working Papers on Fiscal Imbalance. http://www.queensu.ca/iigr/sites/webpublish.queensu.ca.iigrwww/files/files/WorkingPapers/fiscalImb/Stevenson.pdf.

Théret, Bruno. 1999. "Regionalism and Federalism: A Comparative Analysis of the Regulation of Economic Tensions between Regions by Canadian and American Federal Intergovernmental Transfer Programmes." *International Journal of Urban and Regional Research* 23 (3): 479–512. http://dx.doi.org/10.1111/1468-2427.00209.

Usher, Dan. 1995. *The Uneasy Case for Equalization Payments*. Vancouver: The Fraser Institute.

Wallin, Bruce A. 1998. *From Revenue Sharing to Deficit Sharing: General Revenue Sharing and Cities*. Washington, DC: Georgetown University Press.

Watts, Ronald L. 1987. "The American Constitution in Comparative Perspective: A Comparison of Federalism in the United States and Canada." *Journal of American History* 74 (3): 769–92. http://dx.doi.org/10.2307/1902152.

Watts, Ronald L. 1999. *The Spending Power in Federal Systems: A Comparative Analysis*. Kingston: Institute for Intergovernmental Relations.

Watts, Ronald L. 2008. *Comparing Federal Systems*. 3rd ed. Montréal and Kingston: McGill-Queen's University Press for the Institute of Intergovernmental Affairs.

Zuberi, Dan. 2006. *Differences That Matter: Social Policy and the Working Poor in the United States and Canada*. Ithaca: Cornell University Press.

two

The Politics of Equalization

Introduction

The previous chapter explained the creation and the evolution of equalization in Canada, from 1957 to the end of the 1990s. Although there were many changes made to the program in that period, equalization seldom explicitly entered the political arena. However, for a span of about five years in the mid-2000s, equalization became explicitly entangled with the politics of Canadian federalism and the source of high profile intergovernmental conflict.

In this chapter, we discuss how this happened and explain why equalization in Canada presents potential for being politicized. Objective conditions such as the extent of the uneven geographical distribution and fluctuating prices of non-renewable natural resources such as oil and gas do not alone account for this potential, although these factors are significant. We suggest that the program's governance structure, resting as it does on federal executive discretion, is at the heart of this potential for politicization. Also important is the that the competitive dynamic of Canadian federalism features strong provincial governments not afraid to challenge Ottawa. Moreover, some widely held perceptions about the equalization program fuel acrimonious debate once it moves to the centre of the political agenda.

This chapter explores the more contemporary politics of equalization in the twenty-first century with a focus on the Martin (2003–06) and the Harper years (2006–15), a time when the federal program became a highly contentious issue. We also provide an analysis of the factors explaining why equalization can sometimes become a salient political issue and a source of significant intergovernmental conflict. In the final section, we examine some reform options and evaluate what these alternatives would mean for the politicization potential of equalization.

The political debate over equalization:
The Martin and early Harper years

As suggested in the previous chapter, before the mid-2000s, equalization had seldom been a highly contentious political issue in Canada, even during the early Chrétien years (1993–97) when austerity dominated federal politics (Milne 1998).[1] In the 1990s, the federal government effectively kept equalization away from partisan politics by managing it largely at the bureaucratic level. Intergovernmental relations around equalization were handled by civil servants rather than elected officials. In the aftermath of the 1995 federal budget, which suddenly and unilaterally cut transfers to the provinces by merging Established Programs Financing (EPF) and the Canada Assistance Plan (CAP) into the Canada Health and Social Transfer (CHST), the premiers attacked the federal government for effectively reducing resources available to their provinces to fund health care and social services. Everything remained quiet on the equalization front, even as Ottawa and the provinces were negotiating a Social Union Framework Agreement (SUFA) that was to specify, among other things, the role of the federal government in social policy and intergovernmental mechanisms for social policy coordination and cooperation.[2]

A few years later, however, when the provinces challenged the federal government over what they argued was a structural fiscal imbalance favouring Ottawa (a process initiated by Québec, as explained in the previous chapter), equalization was made part of the political debate. The 2002 report of Québec's *Commission sur le déséquilibre fiscal* criticized the federal equalization program for the unpredictable nature of annual payments to qualifying provinces and the limiting impact of the five-province norm on fiscal redistribution that had been in place since the 1980s (Commission on Fiscal Imbalance 2002, 14). The report also stated that provinces should always be consulted before the federal government enacted changes to the equalization program.

In the early 2000s, pressure to reform the equalization program, specifically in a way that would boost the total annual sums paid out to recipient provinces, increased because of two crucial trends. First, during this period, the federal government ran large budget surpluses. As stated in the 2001 federal budget, for instance, "The federal government recorded a budgetary surplus of $17.1 billion in 2000–01. This is the largest annual surplus since Confederation and the fourth consecutive annual surplus, following surpluses of $3.5 billion in 1997–98, $2.9 billion in 1998–99 and $12.3

---

1 The following sections draw on Lecours and Béland (2010).
2 Québec did not sign SUFA, as the PQ found the agreement too centralizing (Noël 2000).

billion in 1999–2000" (Department of Finance Canada 2001, 11). Second, the total amount of equalization payments was decreasing. Total payments for 2000–01 ($10.9 billion) were expected to fall to $8.9 billion the following year as a result of a major economic slowdown in Ontario and tax cuts enacted in several provinces (Expert Panel on Equalization and Territorial Formula Financing 2006, 23). This anticipated decline in equalization payments would particularly affect Québec, then the largest recipient province.

The decrease in the equalization pool was not the only contentious aspect of the equalization program. The problem of the treatment of revenues from non-renewable natural resources such as oil and gas was also resurfacing. At the time, fiscal federalism scholar Tom Courchene claimed that Saskatchewan was the victim of "confiscatory equalization" (Courchene 2004). The basic problem alluded to was that Saskatchewan would see its equalization entitlements reduced by more than the increase in its oil and gas revenues. As Courchene (2004) put it, "In fiscal year 2000–01 Saskatchewan's energy revenues totalled $1.04 billion, or just over $1,000 per capita. However, these energy revenues triggered even larger decreases in Saskatchewan's equalization entitlements, over $1.13 billion, representing an average tax-back rate on Saskatchewan's energy revenues of 108 percent" (2). Even more frustrating for the Saskatchewan government was the fact that the equalization entitlements of two other oil producing provinces, Newfoundland and Labrador and Nova Scotia, were protected from the so-called equalization clawback on energy resources as a result of deals (the Atlantic Accords) struck with the federal government in 1985.

The crucial factor that pulled equalization into the Canadian political debate, however, was the plight of the federal Liberal government at the time. When Martin succeeded Chrétien as prime minister in late 2003, many observers were predicting another decade of Liberal hegemony, as the former finance minister was generally considered more popular than his predecessor. Yet, very soon, the Martin government found itself in political trouble, primarily as a result of the sponsorship scandal,[3] which weakened the standing of the Liberals in the polls. This weakness made it easier for premiers seeking more money from Ottawa to put pressure on the Martin government in several areas, from health care to equalization. During the 2004 federal electoral campaign, Martin came under direct pressure from Premier Danny Williams, "who asked for 100 per cent of Newfoundland and Labrador's share of royalties without any equalization payment clawback" (Dawson 2004). In fact, Conservative leader Stephen Harper had

---

3 The "sponsorship scandal" involved abuses of power and mismanagement around a program aimed at promoting the Canadian "brand" in Québec.

already promised to end the "offshore clawback" by excluding oil revenues from the calculation of provincial fiscal capacity. Thus, when Premier Williams proposed that the "clawback" be the subject of a refund on the part of the federal government, Prime Minister Martin agreed (Clancy 2011, 246).

The financing of the health care system became a huge issue during this 2004 electoral campaign, and Martin famously promised to fix health care "for a generation." The Liberals won the most seats in the 2004 election but fell short of a majority and subsequently formed a minority government. After appointing his cabinet, Martin rapidly struck an agreement with the provinces on health care funding. During the discussions with the provinces, however, it became clear that Québec would not accept any health care deal without an increase in equalization payments. More money for health care, after all, did not mean much if it was to be offset by lower equalization payments. Alongside other receiving provinces, therefore, Québec pushed for equalization reform. Because the health care agreement with the provinces seemed so crucial to the future electoral chances of the Liberal Party, Martin felt compelled to act on the equalization front. Thus, immediately after striking a deal with the provinces on health care funding in September 2004, he announced a new framework for equalization.

The main feature of the new framework was the establishment of a fixed pool of at least $10 billion a year for equalization. The idea behind the fixed-pool rule was to stabilize the financing of the equalization program and, therefore, contribute to the sustainability of the federal budget. For recipient provinces, however, payments to individual units under the fixed-pool rule would become highly unpredictable. With a fixed pool, equalization became a zero-sum game among recipient provinces, as an increase in the payment for one province would mean a decrease for another. The new framework also generated an apparent fairness problem because the post-equalization fiscal capacity of Newfoundland (then a recipient province) became higher than the fiscal capacity of Ontario (then a non-recipient province).

Moreover, the new framework did not address the grievances of resource-rich provinces because the calculation of provincial fiscal capacity still took revenues from non-renewable resources into consideration (Lecours and Béland 2010).[4] This inclusion was especially problematic for two provinces, Newfoundland and Nova Scotia, both saddled with heavy

---

4 Provinces also had a variety of more technical concerns regarding equalization, for example, the issue of property tax measurement.

debts. Then Newfoundland Premier Danny Williams took a particularly aggressive stance toward Prime Minister Martin, as he sought to renegotiate the 1985 Atlantic Accord between Ottawa and his province that had provided for only partial compensation in equalization payment reductions stemming from increased revenue of offshore resources. Premier Williams sought 100 per cent compensation without any limits or caps, something he felt Prime Minister Martin had promised previously. When the federal government balked at his request, Williams promptly had all the Canadian flags lowered from provincial buildings, a highly publicized move (Dunn 2005). In the end, the fragility of his minority government (and a specific concern with the three Newfoundland swing ridings of St. John's North, St. John's South, and Bonavista-Exploits) led Prime Minister Martin to sign new offshore accords guaranteeing both Newfoundland and Nova Scotia 100 per cent protection on equalization payments for eight years.

The new framework had come with the commitment to have an expert review of the equalization program. In March 2005, having endured and still facing sharp criticism over equalization, the Martin government officially announced the creation of the Expert Panel on Equalization and Territorial Formula Financing, which was tasked with reviewing these two federal programs and outlining reform options to improve them.

Chaired by former Alberta senior civil servant Al O'Brien, the panel issued its report to the new minority Conservative government of Stephen Harper in May 2006. The report made several recommendations that addressed key issues related to the equalization program. First, the report suggested abandoning the fixed-pool approach in favour of a formula-driven determination of the total equalization allotment. Second, the panel recommended that the equalization formula consider the fiscal capacity of all 10 provinces, instead of retaining the five-province standard that had previously been used. Third, the report proposed that half of provincial non-renewable resource revenues should be taken into consideration in the calculation of provincial fiscal capacity. Finally, the report suggested that "[a] cap be implemented to ensure that, as a result of equalization, no receiving province ends up with a fiscal capacity greater than that of the lowest non-receiving province" (Expert Panel on Equalization and Territorial Formula Financing 2006, 7).[5]

The panel's report displeased resource-rich provinces. The 50 per cent inclusion of natural resource revenue and, especially, the cap would mean

---

5 In 2006, another report on fiscal federalism was released. Commissioned by the Council of the Federation, this report focused on the broad issue of "fiscal imbalance." Yet, tellingly, the report featured one chapter on equalization policy (Gagné and Stein 2006).

a so-called clawback. In Newfoundland, Premier Danny Williams said the report gave "Newfoundland and Labrador a sledgehammer over the head" (Laghi 2006). However, Premier Williams seemed reassured by the fact that the new prime minister, Stephen Harper, had previously campaigned on the full exclusion of resource revenue from equalization. Saskatchewan Premier Lorne Calvert stated that he was "very disappointed" with the report and that "if these recommendations were to be followed, they would penalize the people of Saskatchewan" (Laghi 2006). As for the premiers of Alberta and Ontario, two non-receiving provinces at that time, both claimed they would oppose any expansion of the equalization program.

Nevertheless, the recommendations of the expert panel formed the core of the reform of the equalization program subsequently outlined by Prime Minister Harper, who took office in early February 2006 at the helm of a minority government. Implementing the report commissioned by the previous Liberal government made sense for the new prime minister, who sought to appear non-partisan over this controversial issue. From a political standpoint, implementing the recommendations meant more money for Québec, a province the Conservatives were courting at the time in an effort to secure a majority government at the next federal election. In an attempt to reduce opposition in resource-rich provinces, Harper allowed the provinces to choose between the 0 and 50 per cent inclusion of resource revenue, as a new cap would make sure that equalization payments would not push a province's fiscal capacity above that of any of the non-receiving provinces (Lecours and Béland 2010). Newfoundland and Nova Scotia were also given the option of remaining within the previous equalization framework.[6]

Nevertheless, resource-rich provinces strongly criticized the Conservative government's decision to implement most of the report's recommendations and accused Harper of having broken his promise to exclude resource revenue from the calculation of fiscal capacity altogether. For example, Premier Danny Williams took out a full-page advertisement in the *Globe and Mail* to denounce Harper for not having kept his promise. Saskatchewan Premier Lorne Calvert called the implementation of a cap on equalization payments a "betrayal" (Scoffield 2007). In June, Calvert announced that his province would launch a lawsuit against the federal government over equalization payments (CBC News 2007). Federal politicians also weighed in on equalization policy. Finance Minister Jim Flaherty belittled previous Liberal "side deals" on resource revenues (Campbell 2006), and Liberal leader Stéphane

---

6 Nova Scotia opted to go into the new system while Newfoundland no longer qualified for equalization payment starting in 2008.

Dion denounced the prime minister for having broken an electoral prom-ise on the exclusion of natural resources from the equalization (CTV News 2007).

In 2008, the global financial market crisis changed the fiscal outlook for all governments. This economic crisis triggered major changes in the cat-egories of recipient and non-recipient provinces and brought more politi-cal discontent over the equalization program. In fact, by that year, as the result of a strong decline of Ontario's manufacturing sector (particularly the automobile industry), it was expected that, starting in 2010–11, Ontario would qualify for equalization payments (TD Bank Financial Group 2008). Premier Dalton McGuinty expressed frustration over Ontario not receiving equalization for another two years, in spite of its descent into recession in 2008–09. McGuinty demanded the "end [of the] outdated federal equaliza-tion program" (Shuffelt 2008).

In a context where federal surpluses were replaced by deficits, equal-ization as a political issue gradually lost a lot of its salience. This loss of salience became particularly clear once Prime Minister Harper was able to form a majority government in the aftermath of the May 2011 federal election.

The Conservative government's approach to federalism, so-called open federalism, consisted of having each level of government operate within its own spheres of constitutional jurisdiction. Viewing these spheres as "water-tight," the Conservative government saw little point in calling first min-isters' meetings or participating in multilateral intergovernmental forums. Equalization, as a purely federal responsibility, represented a program the Harper government sought to administer on its own. Simultaneously, Ontario's qualifying for payments for the first time presented important implications for the costs of the program, considering the province's large population (nearly 12.9 million residents in 2011).

In this context, the federal government implemented two reforms to control overall equalization costs. First, it changed how the cap was determined. In the equalization program's original 2007 form, equalization payments to a province would stop once the fiscal capacity of a recipient province caught up with the fiscal capacity of the "poorest" non-recipient province, which at that time was Ontario.

> [W]ith no change in definition, once Ontario was no longer a non-recipient, the fiscal-capacity cap would be set by British Columbia and be much higher.... However, the federal government redefined the fiscal-capacity cap as the average of the sum of equalization recipients' (a) fiscal capacity ..., (b) their remaining 50 per cent

of natural resource revenues per capita, and (c) their equalization payments per capita. The purpose of this redefinition was to avoid a large increase in total payments. (Feehan 2014, 9)

Second, the Conservative government tied the annual increase of the overall equalization pool to the nominal growth of the gross domestic product (GDP). With this change, equalization was turned back into a fixed-pool structure, limiting the overall costs of the program and limiting its capacity to address the consequences of territorial disparities, which tend to increase in times of higher energy prices.

These changes to the equalization program were decided without meaningful consultation with the provinces, in a fashion similar to the 10-year financing scheme for the Canada Health Transfer announced by then Finance Minister Jim Flaherty in 2011, which also featured a transition toward a system that tied increases in federal funding to GDP growth and a strict per capita structure. If the objective behind this unilateral approach was to avoid the type of political drama generated by the high profile intergovernmental meetings witnessed in the Martin years, the objective was definitely achieved. On equalization, in the context of large federal deficits, the reforms destined to limit overall program costs met with only mild protests on the part of the provinces.

After 2008, and for the remaining of the Harper years (2006–15), equalization was no longer a flashpoint in Canadian politics. This development was reinforced by two factors: the advent in 2011 of a Conservative majority government, a situation that reduced the vulnerability of the federal government to provincial pressures, and the fact that the political parties in Ontario, the province most affected by recent changes limiting the overall pool of the program, proved hesitant to make a fuss over equalization for fear that it could be poorly received by its own population, still unaccustomed to the province's "have-not" status. Overall, however, the situation during the mid-2000s suggests that equalization always has the potential to become a contested and controversial political issue. In the next section, we explain why that is so.

Four main factors

Based on this recent history, we argue that four main factors underlie the potential for the politicization of Canada's equalization program: 1) the concentration of non-renewable natural resources in certain provinces and the fluctuation of commodity prices over time, 2) executive discretion as the basic principle of the program's governance, 3) the political strength of provinces within Canadian federalism, and 4) public perceptions of the program (Lecours and Béland 2010).

Natural resources

Many of the political controversies over equalization in Canada involve the question of natural resources, especially non-renewable ones. Two issues are particularly relevant for understanding how natural resources play into the politicization of equalization. The first issue is that non-renewable natural resources such as oil and gas are unevenly distributed across provinces. More specifically, as suggested in Figure 2.1, the sheer concentration of oil in Alberta (and to a lesser extent in Saskatchewan, Newfoundland and Labrador, and Nova Scotia) exacerbates interprovincial disparities in fiscal capacity. Price volatility creates uncertainty about the payments provinces can expect to receive and, therefore, can induce political and intergovernmental tensions.

The intergovernmental conflicts over equalization during the Martin and the early Harper years occurred when oil prices climbed from about $30 a barrel in July 2003 to nearly $75 a barrel in July 2006, and then to more than $145 a barrel in mid-July 2008 before beginning to fall in the

Figure 2.1 Provincial per capita GDP as a percentage of national per capita GDP, 1961–2013

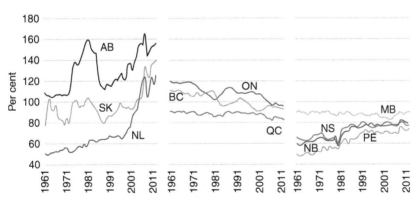

Source: Statistics Canada CANSIM, *Table 051–0001: Estimates of Population; Table 380–0056: Gross Domestic Product (GDP) Indexes; Table 384–0001: Gross Domestic Product (GDP), Income-Based, Provincial Economic Accounts; Table 384–0014: Provincial Gross Domestic Product (GDP); Table 384–0037: Gross Domestic Product, Income-Based, Provincial and Territorial;* and author's calculations. We thank David Péloquin for supplying this graph.

aftermath of the deep economic and financial downturn that hit Canada later that year.

The second issue making natural resources a potential political trigger for equalization is that provinces are, constitutionally, the owners of the resources in their territory. As a result, provincial governments and residents expect to reap the full benefits of these resources. Provinces rich in non-renewable natural resources view their ownership of resources as implying that they should not be penalized (through loss in equalization payments) for revenues generated by their decisions on the rate of exploitation. These provinces have argued that revenues from oil and gas are fundamentally different from all other revenues because oil and gas are non-renewable, that is, not part of an endless revenue stream. This view underpins the claim on the part of the oil- and gas-rich provinces that resource revenues should not be part of the calculation of provincial fiscal capacity. Moreover, inclusion of resource revenues has typically generated a larger overall equalization envelope (at least when the formula determined the equalization pool), an outcome favoured by recipient provinces but opposed by non-recipients. Indeed, non-recipient provinces tend to advocate for a less substantial program, maybe because their residents feel a bigger equalization pool contributes to an overall greater tax burden. In such a context, the federal government is left to arbitrate these contradictory provincial demands (Lecours and Béland 2010).

In Canada, resources are also important for their symbolic value. In Alberta especially, energy resources, particularly oil, explicitly underpin not only the province's economy but also its politics (Tupper, Pratt, and Urquhart 1992, 35–36). The 1980 National Energy Program (NEP), which saw Ottawa impose price control and taxes on oil and gas production, was depicted as an attack against Alberta. Memories of the NEP have helped frame Ottawa as a potential threat and, on the (provincial) right of the political spectrum at least, the equalization program as an attempt to grab the province's oil wealth. These memories are reinforced by the historical experience of Alberta fighting alongside Saskatchewan for control of their natural resources, after their creation as provinces in 1905 (Janigan 2012). For these provinces, resources are highly symbolic markers of provincial autonomy and prosperity. As a result, the federal government's views on resource revenues are highly charged because of their historical symbolism and significance.

Adding to the frustration of oil- and gas-producing provinces in relation to equalization is that many of the monetary benefits hydroelectricity in Québec and Manitoba generates for the provinces' own residents are not factored into the equalization system. For instance, Québec's fiscal capacity would most likely be boosted and equalization payments be decreased if equalization calculations took into account that Hydro-Québec, the province's public utility company, sells electricity at comparatively low prices. This issue is widely reported: for example, Québec artificially lowers its formal fiscal capacity "by allowing provincially owned Hydro-Quebec to charge consumers, especially large industrial ones, a price far below the market value" (Yakabuski 2008, B2). The fact that the structure of equalization in relation to hydroelectricity provides incentives for the Québec government to keep its prices and royalties low (Bernard 2012, 14) becomes a source of frustration for oil producing provinces. In addition to the pure material interests Québec has in reaping the maximum possible benefits from its hydroelectrical power, hydro in that province is as laden historically and symbolically as oil in Alberta because it is associated with the modernizing success and nation-building process of the Quiet Revolution, a period of momentous state-led economic and social development in the province. For these reasons, addressing the issue of hydroelectricity revenue in the equalization formula would almost certainly mean a confrontation with Québec.

Executive discretion

Although the Constitution gives the provinces control over their natural resources, it also places equalization policy in the hands of the federal government. The program has always been the administrative responsibility of the Department of Finance.[7] The constitutional requirement that the federal government make equalization payments to provinces would not prevent the advent of an arm's-length body similar to Australia's Commonwealth Grants Commission, but executive discretion has remained the defining principle for governing equalization in Canada. As a result, equalization is never far away from partisan politics. Federal parties can therefore make competing promises about the program before or after they form the government. These promises are typically informed by

---

7 Technical and strategic information relating to adjustments in the formula are not easily accessible to the public because the 1985 Access to Information Act stipulates that the federal government does not have to disclose information that "could reasonably be expected to be injurious to the conduct by the Government of Canada of federal-provincial affairs" (Article 14) or that represents "advice or recommendations ... for a government institution" (Article 21-a). This secrecy, combined with the complexity of the equalization program, means that "facts" cannot easily serve to tell who is "right" and who is "wrong" in debates about equalization.

political and electoral considerations, and they elicit similar thinking on the part of provincial politicians who see something to gain by engaging their federal counterparts on equalization. The Martin government's treatment of equalization (analyzed previously) is a good example of how the program can quickly become a bargaining chip and a source of political debate and controversy.

In the context of executive discretion over the program, political actors and observers are generally quick to see electoral considerations behind federal decisions about equalization. For instance, the details of the 2007 equalization reform that implemented the main recommendations of the expert panel and that resulted in a boost of funds for Québec became public only a week before a provincial election. Whether it was the case or not, this move was widely perceived as a way to help a federalist party (the Québec Liberal Party) in its struggle with the PQ and to boost support for the Conservative Party in anticipation of the next federal election (Bryden 2007).

Equalization reforms are generally perceived as the federal government picking winners and losers among the 10 provinces. In such a context, provinces whose leaders judge their provinces have been short-changed may decide to come out aggressively against the federal government. This opposition represents a particularly problematic situation for minority governments that struggle to stay in power or seek to attain a majority at the next election. They may be tempted to compensate apparent losers so as to maintain or increase their political support in specific provinces. Although it created much resentment in other parts of the country, the signing of the 2004 offshore accords with Newfoundland and Nova Scotia illustrates this political logic. In fact, these accords appeared to be a way for Prime Minister Martin to shore up electoral support in these two provinces in the wake of the unification of the right through the creation of the Conservative Party of Canada, a political change that posed a direct threat to Liberal power in Ottawa.[8] In sum, executive discretion over equalization policy shapes the politics of equalization in large part because national political parties are sensitive to the support they receive from the provinces, especially when there is a minority government. In reality, the provinces have little to lose by attempting to pressure the federal government to modify the equalization program to their apparent benefit (Stevenson 2007).

---

8 A newspaper article stated that "Finance officials have long opposed the offshore accords, which they see as political bribery aimed at winning votes on the East Coast" (Maher and Jackson 2008, A1).

Federalism and provincial identities

In combination with executive discretion, the structure and nature of Canadian federalism contribute to the potential for the politicization of equalization. In Canada, in contrast to other federal countries such as Germany, provinces do not enjoy the type of regional representation in central institutions that would allow them to shape federal policy making (on equalization or everything else). The only way they can hope to affect federal policies is through directly pressuring the federal government. Because provincial governments have no real competitors when speaking on behalf of their residents, they typically have to be taken very seriously (Simeon 1972; Théret 2002). In fact, premiers tend to assume (and rightly so, predominantly) that, under most circumstances, they will get the support of their residents in a public quarrel with the federal government. This support is, to a large extent, the product of both the strong sense of provincial autonomy and identity that exists in the Canadian federation and, unlike in Australia or the United States, the absence of any effective regional representation at the federal level of government.

Provinces can therefore take an aggressive stance when bargaining with the federal government, especially when they frame issues as intersecting with their interests or identity. As Stevenson (2007) points out regarding fiscal federalism in Canada, "A cynic might say that provincial politicians have nothing to gain, and much to lose, by appearing to be satisfied.... [I]t is far easier and more convenient to attribute the deficiencies of one's highways, hospitals, universities or schools to the distant federal government, which is generally inhibited by constitutional propriety and self-respect, from responding to the verbal abuse that is thrown in its direction, than it is to repair the deficiencies" (2). In this context, criticism of the equalization formula is a hostage to "the politics of blame avoidance," according to which politicians seek to deflect criticisms for unpopular policy decisions or outcomes (Weaver 1986).

The threat by Saskatchewan's New Democratic Party (NDP) government to launch a lawsuit against the federal government for a seemingly unfavourable treatment of the province through the equalization program represented an example of such blame avoidance. Premier Calvert stated at the time that the province's lawsuit "would be based on the sections of the constitution that require the equalization program to be fair and equitable" (CBC News 2007). Calvert kept the threat of a constitutional challenge alive (Whyte 2008), as he was facing a strong electoral challenge from the opposition Saskatchewan Party led by Brad Wall. Ultimately, however, the tactic of picking a fight with Ottawa over equalization did not prevent the electoral defeat of the NDP at the hands of the Saskatchewan Party in the November 2007 provincial elections. In July 2008, Premier Wall's Saskatchewan Party government then dropped the legal challenge against the Conservative federal government initiated by his predecessor (CBC News 2008).

An institutional feature of Canadian politics that facilitates provincial challenges to the federal government on equalization is that, with the exception of the NDP, political parties are organized as separate provincial and federal bodies with limited influence on each other. In some instances, the relationship between "kin" provincial and federal parties is downright frosty (e.g., the Québec Liberal Party and the Liberal Party of Canada have long had quite a tense relationship). The importance of this lack of cooperation at the federal and provincial levels was evident when Newfoundland Premier Danny Williams took on the Harper government during the 2008 federal election for its 2007 equalization reform. Premier Williams, himself leader of the Progressive Conservative Party of Newfoundland and Labrador, urged Newfoundlanders to vote for any candidate but Conservative ones, even launching a website (now defunct)—AnythingButConservative.ca.

Public and media understandings

Equalization is such complex public policy that few Canadians understand how it works (Marchildon 2005). In part, this complexity creates a gap between the actual functioning of equalization and the way it is depicted in public discourse, a discrepancy that can affect the politics of equalization in various ways. Perceptions of the program can facilitate its politicization; in fact, these perceptions can be used for just this purpose. For instance, media reports frequently allude to equalization as a form of welfare for "have-not" provinces. In 2008, when it became official that Ontario would qualify for equalization payments, for example, media headlines described Ontario as a "welfare recipient" (Artuso 2008; Callan 2008). This type of rhetoric suggests that equalization takes money directly from wealthy provinces to send to poorer ones. In reality, the inner workings of the program, which is hardly ever presented in the media or in discussions, is that all Canadian taxpayers, independently of their province of residence, contribute to the equalization pool. But anti-equalization advocates, to fuel opposition to equalization in non-recipient provinces, often characterize the program as moving money from "have" to "have-not" regions.

In Alberta, equalization is viewed through the lens of "Western alienation": the idea that Western provinces do not get a fair deal from existing federal institutions and programs (Lawson 2005). Provincial politicians in Alberta often suggest that equalization involves Alberta sending money to fund other provinces' programs, often considered as overly generous. In the words of Member of the Legislative Assembly (MLA) Ted Morton (2005), "Alberta has watched over $200 billion leave the province over the past four decades in official and unofficial federal transfer programs.... In the current fiscal year, Alberta will watch its $9.3 billion in oil and gas royalty revenues be swallowed up by the $12 billion it will transfer to Ottawa" (3). Presenting the program as taking Alberta's money and sending it elsewhere (to so-called have-not provinces) is bound to nourish antipathy toward equalization and to favour political and intergovernmental conflict around it (Lecours and Béland 2010).

Another understanding of equalization that can trigger controversy over the program is the idea that Québec disproportionately benefits from it, a situation allegedly related to the threat of separation and the need for federal parties to win seats in the province. From this perspective, equalization is frequently understood as a program that funnels enormous amounts of money to Québec for purely partisan electoral reasons. For instance, as early as in 1971, when advocating for dismantling equalization, British Columbia Premier W.A.C. Bennett pointed to the fact that Québec was the main beneficiary of the program: "The Government of Canada has paid out over $5,500,000,000 in equalization payments since their introduction in 1957, and they continue to increase substantially each year. One province, Québec, received 47 per cent of this amount" (Bennett, quoted in Resnick 2000, 23).[9] Media reports often highlight the fact that Québec receives "the lion's share" (Howlett and Carmichael 2008) of equalization money and tend to list these amounts in absolute rather than per capita terms, which accentuates the impression that Québec benefits disproportionally from the program. For example, although it is true that "Québec ... has received $33.4 billion in equalization payments in the past six years" (Campbell 2008), the budgets of other recipient provinces such as New Brunswick, Prince Edward Island, and Manitoba have depended more on equalization payments than Québec on a per capita basis (Perry 1997, 170). Yet, the idea that Québec is by far the main beneficiary of equalization, and that this is the result of its political clout, facilitates the politics of resentment

---

9 Bennett also questioned the usefulness of equalization: "There is little evidence these unconditional grants, which have been paid to certain provincial governments, have increased the relative standard of living of the citizens in the areas in which they have been received" (Bennett, quoted in Resnick 2000, 23).

toward that province. In Alberta conservative politician Ted Morton's words, "Alberta's fate appears to be the opposite of Québec's: the more it contributes financially, the less it receives politically" (Morton 2005, 3).

Equalization and politics: Options for governance reform

The story of equalization in Canada in the 2000s highlights the fact that the program can become a highly salient political question and the centre of fairly serious intergovernmental conflicts. In the Martin and Harper years, the equalization program seemed less the "glue" holding the federation together and more a source of discord and animosity among Canada's governments. This situation was unusual because, for most of the life of the equalization program, discussions and debates around its merits, shortcomings, and problems largely remained confined to experts and bureaucrats. Yet, as this chapter has argued, in part because of the absence of arm's-length governance similar to what is found in Australia and in other federations, Canadian equalization policy presents an inherent potential for politicization.

Most of the factors contributing to this potential for the politicization of the equalization program cannot be controlled. The uneven territorial distribution of oil and gas and the provincial ownership of natural resources are both here to stay. So are the strength of provinces within Canadian federalism and the fierce defence of their autonomy, identity, and interests. Perceptions and understandings of equalization may evolve, but they are the product of a public discourse shaped by different voices, many of which are embedded in the protection and pursuit of specific provincial interests.

To depoliticize equalization, the Government of Canada could decide to have the program governed by an arm's-length agency like Australia's Commonwealth Grants Commission (CGC; Galligan 1995). The CGC is an independent, politically neutral body headed by commissioners who are often former civil servants or prominent economists and supported by a staff of experts. Every year, the CGC, as mandated by the Commonwealth government, proposes a distribution among the states and territories of the revenue from the federal Goods and Services Tax (GST), which serves as a pool for vertical transfers and equalization. Before putting forth its proposal, the CGC seeks information and input from the states and territories, and its staff members typically travel to the various constituent units to meet with their officials. One individual state may feel it should receive more money, but a common proposal from all constituent units is highly improbable considering the zero-sum nature of such an exercise.

The Commonwealth government, for its part, has minimal analytical capacity on equalization issues and provides no distribution proposal of its own.

Unhappy states or territories have few options in the face of a "relativities" distribution they feel disadvantages them. They can challenge the CGC on methodological grounds, but the reputation of the organization for technical expertise and neutrality undermines such efforts. These states and territories can also appeal directly to the federal (Commonwealth) government, but, in absence of an alternative proposal for "relativities" distribution that would be supported by most (if not all) other states and territories, such an appeal typically does not yield any changes. For example, in 2015, the Western Australian government was upset with the CGC's "relativities" because the state's proposed share was very low (about 30 cents for every $1 of GST) at a time when a sudden drop in the price of iron ore compromised its budget. Finding no sympathy among other states (O'Connor 2015), the Western Australian government sought some type of adjustment on the part of the Commonwealth government, but the CGC's recommendation was maintained.

As a result of the CGC's authoritative decision-making role on distributing GST money to the states, equalization has mostly been taken out of politics. Could this governance structure remove some of the politicization potential of Canada's equalization program?

Transplanting an institution embedded in a state's larger political and institutional landscape to another state is always a tricky exercise (Campbell 2004). The strength of provincial identities in Canada means it would be much more difficult for an agency to operate so that its individual commissioners were viewed as adopting a pan-Canadian rather than a specific provincial perspective. In other words, there is a chance that the neutral legitimacy of such a body would be compromised by the dynamics of Canadian federalism. Still, taking decision making about equalization out of the hands of the federal executive presents the potential for depoliticizing equalization, as it would make it harder for federal politicians to use the program directly to feed their electoral strategies, as was sometimes the case during the Martin and the early Harper years.

Despite the fact that an arm's-length agency has often been considered a potential governance option for Canada's equalization program (e.g., by the Expert Panel on Equalization and Territorial Formula Financing [2006, 39]) and that several policy experts (e.g., Joanis [2010]) have advocated its creation, resistance from both the provinces and the federal government must be considered. Provinces prefer to deal directly with the federal government on equalization because they know they can at least attempt to exert political pressure in exchange for a more favourable outcome. In other words, as long as equalization remains subject to federal executive discretion, provinces have the opportunity to voice complaints about equalization decisions to a governing body concerned with politics as much as policy. The federal government, for its part, is most likely loath to relinquish responsibility for the administration of a program that enables its leadership in the federation and its capacity to shape the Canadian identity. A belief, on the part of many important political actors (e.g., the Liberal Party of Canada), that equalization is a fundamental component of Canadian citizenship and a crucial tool for furthering equality and fairness in the country also plays against its administration by an arm's-length agency.

References

Artuso, Antonella. 2008. "We're in Line for Handout." *Toronto Sun*, November 4.

Bernard, Jean-Thomas. 2012. *The Canadian Equalization Program: Main Elements, Achievements and Challenges*. Montréal: L'idée fédérale.

Bryden, Joan. 2007. "Provinces Slam Tories' Fiscal Gap Cure." *Toronto Star*, March 20. https://www.thestar.com/news/2007/03/20/provinces_slam_tories_fiscal_gap_cure.html.

Callan, Eoin. 2008. "Ontario to be a 'Have-Not' Province." *National Post*, November 4.

Campbell, John L. 2004. *Institutional Change and Globalization*. Princeton: Princeton University Press.

Campbell, Murray. 2006. "Flaherty Slams Martin Government's Equalization Deals." *Globe and Mail*, March 11. http://www.theglobeandmail.com/news/national/flaherty-slams-martin-governments-equalization-deals/article1095750/.

Campbell, Murray. 2008. "Ontario Becomes Pauper in a Broken System." *Globe and Mail*, November 4, A1.

CBC News. 2007. "Sask. Will Sue over Equalization: Calvert." *CBC News*, June 13. http://www.cbc.ca/news/canada/saskatchewan/sask-will-sue-over-equalization-calvert-1.679144.

CBC News. 2008. "Sask. Drops Legal Challenge of Equalization." *CBC News*, July 10. http://www.cbc.ca/news/canada/saskatchewan/sask-drops-legal-challenge-of-equalization-1.710727.

Clancy, Peter. 2011. *Offshore Petroleum Politics: Regulation and Risk in the Scotian Basin*. Vancouver: UBC Press.

Commission on Fiscal Imbalance. 2002. *A New Division of Canada's Financial Resources: Report*. Quebec City: Government of Québec. http://www.groupes.finances.gouv.qc.ca/desequilibrefiscal/en/pdf/rapport_final_en.pdf.

Courchene, Thomas J. 2004. "Confiscatory Equalization: The Intriguing Case of Saskatchewan's Vanishing Energy Revenues." *Choices* 10 (2). http://archive.irpp.org/choices/archive/vol10no2.pdf.

CTV News. 2007. "Accord Dispute Creates Dissent in Harper Cabinet." *CTV News*, June 11).

Dawson, Anne. 2004. "Martin Visits Every Region on the Campaign's Last Day." *CanWest News*, June 27.

Department of Finance Canada. 2001. *The Budget Plan 2001*. Ottawa: Department of Finance.

Dunn, Christopher. 2005. "Why Williams Walked, Why Martin Balked: The Atlantic Accord Dispute in Perspective." *Policy Options*, February 1. http://policyoptions. irpp.org/magazines/canada-in-the-world/why-williams-walked-why-martin-balked-the-atlantic-accord-dispute-in-perspective/.

Expert Panel on Equalization and Territorial Formula Financing. 2006. *Achieving a National Purpose: Putting Equalization Back on Track*. Ottawa: Expert Panel on Equalization and Territorial Formula Financing.

Feehan, James P. 2014. *Canada's Equalization Formula: Peering inside the Black Box ... and Beyond*. SPP Research Paper No. 7 (24). Calgary: The School of Public Policy, University of Calgary.

Gagné, Robert, and Janice Gross Stein. 2006. *Reconciling the Irreconcilable: Addressing Canada's Fiscal Imbalance*. Ottawa: Council of the Federation.

Galligan, Brian. 1995. *A Federal Republic: Australia's Constitutional System of Government*. Melbourne: Cambridge University Press. http://dx.doi.org/10.1017/CBO9781139084932.

Howlett, Karen, and Kevin Carmichael. 2008. "Struggling Ontario Joins Have-Not Ranks." *Globe and Mail*, November 4. http://www.theglobeandmail.com/news/national/struggling-ontario-joins-have-not-ranks/article662588/.

Janigan, Mary. 2012. *Let the Eastern Bastards Freeze in the Dark: The West versus the Rest since Confederation*. Toronto: Knopf Canada.

Joanis, Marcelin. 2010. "Péréquation: Les plaques tectoniques du déséquilibre fiscal horizontal sont en mouvement." *Policy Options*, May 1, 41–45. http://policyoptions. irpp.org/magazines/the-fault-lines-of-federalism/perequation-les-plaques-tectoniques-du-desequilibre-fiscal-horizontal-sont-en-mouvement/.

Laghi, Brian. 2006. "Ottawa's Blue-Ribbon Panel Backs Enriched Equalization." *Globe and Mail*, June 6. http://www.theglobeandmail.com/news/national/ottawas-blue-ribbon-panel-backs-enriched-equalization-program/article709784/.

Lawson, Robert J. 2005. "Understanding Alienation in Western Canada: Is 'Western Alienation' the Problem? Is Senate Reform the Cure?" *Journal of Canadian Studies / Revue d'études canadiennes* 39 (2): 127–55.

Lecours, André, and Daniel Béland. 2010. "Federalism and Fiscal Policy: The Politics of Equalization in Canada." *Publius: The Journal of Federalism* 40 (4): 569–96. http://dx.doi.org/10.1093/publius/pjp030.

Maher, Stephen, and David Jackson. 2008. "Millions Coming Our Way: Reports on Offshore Windfalls Say N.S. Could Get up to $850 Million." *Chronicle-Herald*, July 9, A1.

Marchildon, Gregory P. 2005. "Understanding Equalization: Is It Possible?" *Canadian Public Administration* 48 (3): 420–28. http://dx.doi.org/10.1111/j.1754-7121.2005. tb00233.x.

Milne, David. 1998. "Equalization and the Politics of Restraint." In *Equalization: Its Contribution to Canada's Fiscal and Economic Progress*, edited by Robin W. Boadway and Paul A.R. Hobson, 175–204. Kingston, ON: John Deutsch Institute for the Study of Economic Policy, Queen's University.

Morton, Ted. 2005. *Equality or Asymmetry? Alberta at the Crossroads*. Asymmetry Series No. 5. Kingston, ON: Queen's University School of Policy Studies.

Noël, Alan. 2000. "Without Quebec: Collaborative Federalism with a Footnote." *Policy Matters / Enjeux publics* 1 (2). http://irpp.org/wp-content/uploads/2014/09/pmvol1n02.pdf.

O'Connor, Andrew. 2015. "GST Share: States and Territories "Bloody Greedy" WA Treasurer Says." ABC News, April 10. http://www.abc.net.au/news/2015-04-10/gst-share-states-bloody-greedy-wa-treasurer-mike-nahan-says/6383764.

Perry, David B. 1997. *Financing the Canadian Federation, 1867 to 1995: Setting the Stage for Change.* Toronto: Canadian Tax Foundation.

Resnick, Philip. 2000. *The Politics of Resentment: British Columbia Regionalism and Canadian Unity.* Vancouver: UBC Press.

Scoffield, Heather. 2007. "'C'est fini,' to Bickering on Imbalance, Flaherty Says." *Globe and Mail*, March 20. http://www.theglobeandmail.com/news/national/cest-fini-to-bickering-on-imbalance-flaherty-says/article17993064/.

Shuffelt, Tim. 2008. "Time to End Outdated Federal Equalization Program: McGuinty." *Ottawa Citizen*, May 9.

Simeon, Richard. 1972. *Federal-Provincial Diplomacy: The Making of Recent Policy in Canada.* Toronto: University of Toronto Press.

Stevenson, Garth. 2007. "Fiscal Federalism and the Burden of History." Paper presented at Queen's Institute of Intergovernmental Relations' conference, Fiscal Federalism and the Future of Canada, Kingston, ON, 28–29 September 2006. In Working Papers on Fiscal Imbalance. http://www.queensu.ca/iigr/sites/webpublish.queensu.ca.iigrwww/files/files/WorkingPapers/fiscalImb/Stevenson.pdf.

TD Bank Financial Group. 2008. *Ontario Poised to Collect Equalization in 2010–2011.* Toronto: TD Bank Financial Group.

Théret, Bruno. 2002. *Protection sociale et fédéralisme: L'Europe dans le miroir de l'Amérique du Nord.* Montréal: Presses de l'Université de Montréal.

Tupper, Allan, Larry Pratt, and Ian Urquhart. 1992. "The Role of Government." In *Government and Politics in Alberta* edited by Allan Tupper and Roger Gibbins, 31–66. Edmonton: University of Alberta Press.

Weaver, R. Ken. 1986. "The Politics of Blame Avoidance." *Journal of Public Policy* 6 (4): 371–98. http://dx.doi.org/10.1017/S0143814X00004219.

Whyte, John D. 2008. "Province Has Good Reason to Go to Court." *Leader-Post*, April 10.

Yakabuski, Konrad. 2008. "Have-Not Status Is All about Gaming the Rules." *Globe and Mail*, November 6, B2.

three
The Economics of Equalization

Introduction

The economic rationale for equalization payments from a national level of government to subnational jurisdictions in a decentralized federation framework stems primarily from the desire to realize the benefits from decentralization, without suffering the potential negative consequences. There are good economic reasons that a decentralized form of government such as federalism is desirable, but there are also potential negative side effects, such as inefficient migration as well as vertical and horizontal fiscal gaps. Before this chapter describes the economic rationale for equalization payments, it is thus useful to present the economic rationale for fiscal decentralization.

Following the presentation of the economic rationales for a decentralized federation and, in this context, the economic basis for equalization payments, we discuss some potential negative economic effects of equalization payments. We turn then to some descriptive statistics regarding equalization payments to the provinces and examine whether key relationships are consistent with expectations arising from theoretical considerations. The final section notes outstanding and ongoing issues related to the federal equalization program in Canada.

The economic logic of decentralized federations

A key rationale for decentralization lies in the possible efficiency gains in the provision of public goods and services, reflected in Oates's (1972) "decentralization theorem." The principle is that, unless tastes and preferences are completely homogenous across a country, there are benefits to having decentralized government institutions. It is argued that subnational (in Canada, provincial) governments can be more attuned to local priorities, can be better held accountable to their local populations, and will have lower information costs in discerning local needs and the means of meeting them than would a more remote national government. The decentralization theorem thus posits that decentralization results in more efficient public goods provision at the subnational level, compared with all public goods being provided at the national level. These public goods are goods and services that are provided either inefficiently or not at all by the market, due to their characteristics.[1] Generally, they can be used or consumed jointly without one person's use affecting that of others, such as a lighthouse, public art, public safety services, or provincial parks.

Oates (2005) credits the development of the decentralization theorem, central to what he calls first generation fiscal federalism, to the Arrow-Musgrave-Samuelson (AMS) perspective of public economics of the 1950s and 1960s. This perspective is the result of two papers published by Paul Samuelson in 1954 and 1955 on the nature of public goods (Samuelson 1954, 1955), the 1969 conceptualization by Kenneth Arrow of the roles of the public and private sectors (Arrow 1969), and Richard Musgrave's case for public finance with an active role for government in correcting market failure, achieving an equitable income distribution, and stabilizing the macroeconomy (Musgrave 1959).

The underlying assumption of the decentralization theorem is that governments seek to maximize the social welfare of their constituents, not in the least because of electoral pressures in a democracy (Oates 2005; Vo 2010). Public goods vary in the geographic scope over which their benefits accrue and in the economies of scale in their production. A "perfect mapping" of government level and public goods provision is one in which the jurisdiction of a level of government corresponds to the area over which the benefits of the public goods are realized (Oates 2005). Spillovers and overlapping benefit areas can be addressed through the use of intergovernmental transfers. The geographic mobility of individuals, also known as "Tiebout sorting," will facilitate the matching of individuals' public goods preferences with the various public goods bundles available across subnational jurisdictions (Tiebout 1956). Households are likely to be heterogeneous in their preferences with respect to bundles of public goods (at a constant tax price), and thus they will be able to sort themselves into the locations that match their preferences (Tiebout 1956). Households, then, will be better off than if public services (and associated taxes) were the same in every jurisdiction. This idea must be qualified by the consideration of economies of size and scale. If the subnational jurisdiction is too "small" (in geographic or population size) to realize economies of size for a particular good or service, then the cost per person of providing that good or service at that particular level is higher than it would otherwise be.

---

1 For a more complete definition of public goods, see Rosen, Wen, and Snoddon (2012, 50).

A second main economic advantage of decentralization is the resulting competition among subnational governments (Hamlin 1991; Qian and Roland 1998; Winer and Hettich 2010). If one subnational government is inefficient in its provision of public goods in terms of their tax costs relative to a neighbouring jurisdiction, then its population may relocate in the direction of greater efficiency. Individuals will "vote with their feet," a variation of the Tiebout sorting already described above. The threat of inter-jurisdictional migration is an important mechanism for holding sub-national governments accountable for their policies. Subnational govern-ments, it is argued, will be motivated to provide public goods efficiently because of the threat of losing their constituents.

An emerging "second-generation theory of fiscal federalism" relies more on public choice and political economy models (Oates 2005, 349; Vo 2010). Political actors pursue their own objectives, a behaviour that is constrained in a decentralized government setting. Subnational govern-ments pursuing their own objectives might consist of them maximizing their budgets, power, and influence (Brennan and Buchanan 1980). Where there are subnational governments that must compete to retain and attract population, this behaviour is constrained. If a subnational government does not provide good government at a competitive tax price, it faces the threat or reality of population out-migration. The more decentralized govern-ments are disciplined by competition, the less likely they are to pursue their own objectives at the expense of their citizens. Nevertheless, as in the decentralization theorem, differences across subnational units and govern-ment functions can have benefits that extend beyond the particular juris-diction being targeted. The presence and size of the spillovers of benefits or costs from one jurisdiction into others are still important considerations in assessing the relative merits of centralized and decentralized governments (Besley and Coate 2003). Where government functions have significant benefits (or costs) in neighbouring jurisdictions, or nationally, the benefits of decentralizing these functions are reduced.

The economic justification for a decentralized government is thus well established. However, as suggested in Chapter 1, it is equally acknowledged that decentralization introduces challenges, including vertical and hori-zontal fiscal gaps between levels of government (Bird and Tarasov 2004). Horizontal gaps refer to differences in either tax bases or costs of providing public services across subnational units. They can result in varying net fiscal benefits (NFB) across jurisdictions. That is, the quantity or quality of public services provided to residents, per own tax dollar, can be dif-ferent across subnational units (Boadway and Flatters 1982a; Vaillancourt and Bird 2004). Vertical gaps occur, as described in Chapter 1, when "the federal government's tax sources are much greater than its expenditure responsibilities whereas, in the provinces, precisely the opposite is the case" (Atkinson et al. 2013, 62).

The economic rationale for equalization payments

The economic rationale for equalization payments in the decentralized federations to be discussed here arises mainly from two main concerns—fiscally induced migration and horizontal inequity.[2] In both cases, the theoretical bases are strong and warrant serious and continuing consideration, even though empirical evidence remains mixed. These concepts underlie the design and commitment to equalization programs in most decentralized countries, and should thus be well understood. The absence of conclusive empirical "proof" of the nature of the influence of these concepts does not negate their value and importance in understanding equalization programs, pointing instead to the need for continuing and improved empirical investigation.

Fiscally induced migration

Fiscally induced migration, which may be one of the unintended negative effects of a decentralized government, is a result of the fiscal horizontal gaps that decentralization generates. Fiscally induced migration is a result not of fiscal policy but rather of underlying differences in the fiscal capacity of subnational units. The basic assumption is that many individuals are at least somewhat mobile, and they make choices regarding where they live and whether or not they are prepared to move from where they live to another location or province. These choices will include comparing expectations of, among other things, employment prospects, income levels, climate, culture, housing costs, family connections, and the available public services relative to the tax cost of living in that province. Migration in expectation of better wages or employment prospects is considered efficient migration, as explained below. If, however, the migration is the result of moving to higher net fiscal benefits, it is considered inefficient. Net fiscal benefits (NFBs) is a term referring to the gap between the public services provided and the taxes due. NFBs may be different across provinces because of differences

---

2 Dahlby (2005, 2011) quite correctly identifies a third economic justification for equalization in a federal system, namely the potential to design equalization payments in order to equalize the marginal cost of public funds across subnational governments. This third justification will not be discussed here due to the complexity of the argument.

in tax revenue bases. Interprovincial differences in NFBs can result in fiscally induced migration—migration in response to better public services per tax dollar paid (Boadway and Flatters 1982a, 1982b). Federal equalization grants for the purpose of reducing or avoiding fiscally induced migration will increase efficiency.

To understand what is meant by fiscally induced migration, why it might be a concern, and why equalization payments may be intended to avoid or reduce it, we need to first understand what efficient, or economically desirable, interprovincial migration consists of. Efficient interprovincial migration requires labour to move in the direction of higher productivity, measured by the value of the output produced. If labour productivity is higher in one location than another, then the total value of national production, the size of the national "pie," as it were, will be increased if labour moves into the higher productivity location. This labour productivity, or more precisely the productivity of the incremental or last worker, is known as the value of the marginal product (VMP). This is simply the value of the contribution that the marginal (the last or the next) worker makes to the total value of production in that location.

As labour moves from lower VMP to higher VMP locations, the productivity levels in both the origin and destination will change. This is the fundamental principle of diminishing marginal productivity. If all else is constant, an increase in the number of workers (a supply shift to the right in the text box, Labour Market Equilibrium, on next page) will lead to a gradual reduction in the value of the VMP that an additional worker contributes. Similarly, as the supply of labour decreases in a region due to out-migration, that region's VMP increases. The process of migration, then, while increasing the total value of national production, will continue until the VMP in the two locations is equal and there is no longer any employment-related incentive to move. This is efficient migration because it increases the total value of production in the nation.

While workers are not likely aware of the details of their VMP, they will know the wage, or income, in their current employment (as well as the local unemployment rate), and they will have some expectations regarding what is likely in terms of wages and employment in a competing location. Wages are generally a reasonable representation of VMP; wage differences are likely important signals that individuals respond to in their location and migration decisions. Firms will pay their employees no more than what they contribute in value to the activity of the enterprise, and if they pay them less, they risk losing employees because they could migrate to a place that will pay them their VMP. So we treat VMP and wages as being very closely related.

Labour Market Equilibrium

The graphs below illustrate how labour market equilibrium is achieved across province A and B. Initially, the wages are higher in province A (W_A) than in province B (W_B). The higher wages (reflecting higher VMP in A) result in labour migration from B to A. As labour moves, the labour supply in B decreases and that in province A increases, denoted in the graphs by the shift of the supply curves. In province B, the shift is from S_{BI} to S_{Be}. In province A, the increase in labour supply as workers move from B to A results in the labour supply shift there from S_{AI} to S_{Ae}. The supply shift continues until the resulting wage, the outcome of supply and demand (VMP), is equalized across provinces (W_e). The amount of labour migration from province B to province A = $(Q_{BI} - Q_{Be}) = (Q_{Ae} - Q_{AI})$.

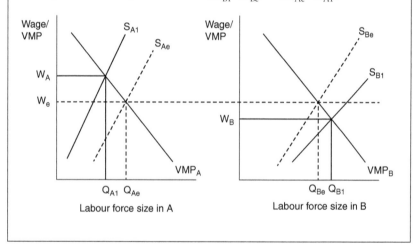

What is described above and illustrated in the text box is a highly stylized version of the migration process. There are costs associated with migration, both monetary and personal, that will also be considered, as well as the stability or security of employment (income earning opportunities) in both origin and destination locations. In reality, there may thus be considerable "stickiness" to labour movements.

In the public finance literature, Buchanan (1950) was the first to advance the argument in favour of central government transfers to subnational units for the purpose of equalizing the fiscal capacities of jurisdictions to avoid inefficient labour mobility due to differences in net fiscal benefits (fiscally induced migration). He argued that the different fiscal capacities of subnational units might result in different public services per tax dollar across jurisdictions. In Canada, for example, wealthier provinces may provide more or better health or education services per tax dollar, thus attracting migrants because of lower costing public services rather than higher productivity (reflected in higher wages). The inefficiency that is created when migration occurs in response to differences in the cost of public services, rather than productivity differences, leads to an overall reduction in social welfare (Buchanan 1950; Bucovetsky 1998). Regions with higher labour productivity may then experience labour shortages, as labour is instead attracted to places with lower costing public services, reducing national output by the production not realized by migration to the high productivity region. Equalization payments may be made both to achieve greater equity across jurisdictions and to correct for the economically inefficient migration that would otherwise occur (Bergvall et al. 2006; Boadway and Flatters 1982a, 1982b; Bucovetsky 1998; Flatters, Henderson, and Mieszkowski 1974; Hercowitz and Pines 1991; Martinez-Vazquez and Boex 2001; Mieszkowski and Toder 1983).

Horizontal equity

The second part of the economic rationale for equalization payments from national to subnational jurisdictions is achieving some measure of horizontal equity. Dahlby (2005) argues that, in the Canadian context, horizontal fiscal equity is an important but not a paramount goal, otherwise a unitary form of government would have been chosen. However, horizontal equity has been a concern in Canada from Canada's inception, as have measures to achieve this equity. In a decentralized country, horizontal equity means, conceptually, that otherwise identical persons should be treated equally in terms of the tax price of public services regardless of where they reside (Boadway 2004). The particular extent to which horizontal equity is desired is not readily determined. In a country as large and heterogeneous as Canada, even though improving horizontal equity may be an ongoing commitment, absolute equity is not likely to be realized.

Boadway (2012) describes horizontal equity as a condition of social citizenship. He argues that, without perfect mobility of the population, residents of rich provinces will have more services per tax dollar than those in poor provinces, violating basic social citizenship equality. Because mobility is less than perfect and the costs of moving (involving both monetary and information acquisition) may be significant, inequality in access to public goods and services is especially concerning. Equalization payments are then intended, in part, to address horizontal inequity because of the imperfect mobility of the population.

Equalization payments for the purposes of addressing horizontal inequities in public services across jurisdictions may take the form of equalizing the revenue capacity of subnational units, rather than equalizing the services directly, especially when there are restrictions on the national government's activities, as is the case in Canada. As described in Chapter 1, the Canadian constitutional basis for equalization payments refers specifically to the "reasonably comparable revenues" to provide "reasonably comparable services." Equalization payments are unconditional grants in that it is entirely up to the provinces to decide how the equalization payments will be used in their respective jurisdictions. There is no requirement that the provincial governments use the transfers actually to provide services that are comparable across provinces. To realize the advantages of a decentralized form of government, the Canadian federation has sacrificed perfect equality in the type, quantity, and quality of public services across provinces.

In response to heterogeneous populations, provincial governments will provide different bundles of public services. In addition to the existence of heterogeneous populations, the constitutional division of powers also precludes the federal government from interfering with how the provinces carry out their obligations in their areas of jurisdiction. The grants can thus only be permissive in promoting horizontal equity in public services and taxation.

Included in considerations of improved horizontal equity as a rationale for equalization payments is the insurance that such payments afford against the occasional shocks that disproportionately affect some provinces (Boadway 2012). Equalization payments funded by the federal government can provide the advantage of pooling risks and of delivering better access to capital markets to improve horizontal equity.

Potential negative effects of equalization payments

Although an economic case can be made for equalization payments in Canada, there is considerable debate about the effectiveness of these payments. There is some evidence that equalization payments may not be needed to equalize provincial fiscal capacities, that they may have an effect but not the desired one, or even that they do harm. Understanding these potential challenges is important when assessing Canada's equalization program.

First, we address the question of whether the payments are needed. It is possible that regional differences in fiscal capacity (often closely related to economic outcomes in a region or province) may be fully capitalized into wages, rents, and prices so that there is "nothing to equalize" (Courchene 2005). If larger tax bases in wealthier regions, for example, coincide with higher wages and higher costs of providing public services, then the higher revenue in a wealthy province does not translate into higher purchasing power or the ability to provide superior services. That is, fiscal capacity differences are capitalized into differences in wages, rents, and prices—thus there is no equalization required. Courchene (2005) points out that the Canadian equalization formula assumes that there is no capitalization. It assumes that an increase in a province's per capita revenue allows that province to provide proportionally more public goods and services to its residents. But to the extent that prices of public goods and services change with higher per capita revenue, this does not follow. Courchene (2005) provides empirical evidence about the extent to which wage levels in the provinces are positively related to revenues, such that the purchasing power (in terms of public goods provided) of higher revenues is reduced. Though it is unlikely that revenue differences are fully capitalized into higher prices, assuming there is no capitalization (as the Canadian program does) is probably also unrealistic. If the capitalization were accounted for, we would have a better idea of what revenues really represent in terms of the public goods and services they can buy.

Investigations of the direct effects of equalization payments on the distribution of well-being are also informative. Tarroux (2012) revealed that, for most empirical scenarios, equalization payments in Canada have an ambiguous impact on the distribution of the well-being that they are intended to address and that, under some scenarios, equalization payments can actually worsen the inequity of well-being across provinces. Watson (1986) also estimates that the implied welfare gains of equalization payments are very small in Canada.

At the heart of evaluating the effectiveness of equalization payments in preventing or reducing fiscally induced migration is the questions of whether interprovincial migration is at all sensitive to provincial differences in government spending or taxation. If not, then there would be no need for policies and programs (such as equalization) to avert it. The theoretical literature discussed above (Boadway 2004; Buchanan 1950, Bucovetsky 1998; Shah 1997) points to the conditions under which this fiscally induced migration may occur.

In spite of concerted efforts and some rigorous empirical analyses that provide valuable evidence of key relationships, the empirical evidence to support the presence of fiscally induced migration is mixed. On the one hand, weak or non-existent policy-induced interprovincial migration in Canada is reported by Day and Winer (2006), Shaw (1986), and Winer and Gauthier (1982). Mieszkowski and Toder (1983) also estimate that the inefficiencies resulting from a fiscally induced out-migration of capital and labour to natural resource endowed states in the United States would be very small. Bakhshi, Shakeri, Olfert, Partridge, and Weseen (2009) investigate the influence of equalization payments on interprovincial migration from 1982 to 2004, controlling for the persistent relative attributes of the provinces. They find that, at the margin, federal transfers in the form of equalization payments have virtually no impact on net migration patterns. Thus, there is a body of empirical analysis that calls into question the presence of the migration effects of government policy, including equalization payments.

However, researchers using different data and model construction have found empirical evidence that provincial spending does affect migration. Based on the estimation of a model of Canadian interprovincial migration using 1962–81 tax data, Day (1992) finds that migration is influenced by provincial government spending, transfers to persons, and average tax rates. Wilson (2003) shows that migratory flows do respond, albeit sluggishly, to changes in equalization payments, thus leading to welfare gains from Canadian equalization. Shaw (1986) concurs, finding that social security type programs offset "natural" incentives to migrate from low income to high income regions in Canada. Considering overall empirical findings both supporting and refuting the migration effects of government spending, we find weak empirical evidence that interprovincial migration flows respond to either government revenue or expenditure differences. That is, it has not been definitively established that equalization payments are effective in mitigating (questionably existent) fiscally induced migration, though there is reason for vigilance and further investigation.

If equalization payments are not needed or are ineffective but are nevertheless undertaken at considerable public expense, then this use of public funds cannot be defended on efficiency grounds. The relevant question is whether transfer revenue would likely have had a higher return if used for other purposes.

A more sinister outcome is that the equalization payments do have an impact—but not the positive one for which they are designed. There are several potential and unintended negative side effects of federal transfers to provinces, effects that introduce inefficiencies. These may be categorized under the "flypaper effect" or the creation of a "welfare trap."

In general terms, the "flypaper effect" refers to a specific consequence of subnational governments receiving unconditional grants from a central government in a fiscal federation. Conceptually, it is relatively straight-forward to demonstrate that such grants are likely to be spent rather than being passed on to citizens in the form of tax cuts (Dahlby 2011; Gramlich 1977; Hall 2008; Hines and Thaler 1995; Rosen, Wen, and Snoddon 2012). That is, total spending by the subnational government is higher than it would have been if revenues had been raised locally rather than having been received as a grant. In other words, the grant "sticks where it lands"; namely, it stays with the provincial government rather than being passed on to residents. This "sticking where it lands" has spawned the label "flypaper effect." However, one cannot infer that there is a flypaper effect by looking at per capita spending alone. Empirical evidence of a flypa-per effect related to equalization payments, that is, a causal link between higher equalization payments and higher per capita government expendi-ture, requires that all other factors be held constant. Nevertheless, there is considerable empirical evidence that is consistent with the presence of a flypaper effect (Dahlby and Ferede 2016; Grossman 1990; Hamilton 1986; Hines and Thaler 1995; Inman 2008; Kneebone 2012; Logan 1986, Turnbull 1998; Winer 1983).

Research into the flypaper effect in the context of the effects of equal-ization payments in Canada ranges from studies positing simple sugges-tive relationships to rigorous empirical investigations (Courchene 1970; Crowley and O'Keefe 2006a, 2006b; Dahlby and Ferede 2016; Ferede 2014; Kneebone 2012; Shah 1997). The argument is as follows. The arrival of transfers from the federal government directly to residents of the provinces would be just like any other increase in income. We would expect to see the residents' use of the income (the expenditure distribution between private goods and public goods) to be similar to already existing public/private expenditure proportions (Bradford and Oates 1971; Hines and Thaler 1995). When the provincial governments (rather than residents) receive the transfers from the central government, there may be other outcomes. If provincial governments, as a result of receiving federal transfers, increase public spending so that the public/private spending proportion increases, a flypaper effect may be suspected. However, to establish a cause-effect rela-tionship empirically requires a rigorous analysis well beyond simply compar-ing per capita government spending. In the case of Canada's equalization payments, Ferede (2014) finds evidence of a flypaper effect specifically for health spending in Canada, though not for other provincial spend-ing. Similarly, Kneebone (2012) finds empirical evidence that provincial government spending in Canada is greater when the revenue arrives in the form of equalization transfers rather than when it is the result of local taxation—evidence of a flypaper effect. The implied inefficiency is due to the fact that the spending patterns that result from the equalization grant being paid to provincial governments are different from those desired by residents (as reflected in residents' spending patterns if they received the transfer payments directly).

The creation of a "welfare trap" is a second category of the possible negative side effects of equalization payments in Canada. The welfare trap discussion concerns itself with the potential interference of equalization payments in efficient interprovincial migration—migration in the direction of higher productivity (Courchene 1970, 2005). Persistently below average incomes in some regions may be an unintended side effect of federal transfers if receipt of these transfers inadvertently provides incentives for provincial governments to make decisions that maximize transfer receipts at the expense of decisions focused on long-run growth, leading to a greater dependency on such payments. The long-run effect is that the recipient region becomes less and less attractive as a place of residence and investment because of the indirect and unintended fiscal consequences of federal transfers (Dahlby 2002; Glaeser, Kolko, and Saiz 2001; Myers 1990; Polèse and Shearmur 2006).

In the regional economics literature, inadvertently interfering with productivity-enhancing migration is a strong argument against policies that target locations, or "places," rather than people. When transfers are attached to places, they create a barrier to mobility—individuals considering migration could be discouraged from doing so because they would not be able to take the benefits of the place-specific subsidy with them (Bolton 1992; Olfert et al. 2014; Partridge and Rickman 2008). People-based transfers would not interfere with mobility because individuals who are mobile can take the benefits of the transfer with them.

In summary, the empirical evidence in the literature regarding the effects of equalization payments from the federal to the provincial governments in Canada is mixed. This is at least in part because it is difficult to construct the counterfactual situation—what would interprovincial migration, productivity, public goods provision, and inequality have been like in the absence of equalization payments? To a large extent there has always been horizontal fiscal redistribution in Canada. It emerged long before the creation of the equalization program in 1957 (Courchene 1984). Further, the various unintended effects (if present) could be offsetting, such that, for example, equalization payments could both result in distortionary provincial spending and also help to stem fiscally induced migration. Horizontal equity may be achieved at the expense of reduced national productivity because of created barriers to migration, though migration effects are likely different for different age, education, and income cohorts. Although the precise effects of equalization payments are difficult to disentangle, it is important to be aware of what problems these transfers are intended to address, and what are their potential and unintended side effects.

Descriptive statistics on regional inequality and equalization payment effects

This section turns to some simple descriptive data concerning equalization payments in Canada from 1980–81 to 2015–16[3] fiscal year, including payment amounts, the conditions triggering payments, and possible effects. These simple statistics cannot be the basis of conclusions regarding the previously described theoretical or potential effects of equalization payments. That task is well beyond the scope of this chapter. However, they can be instructive by showing whether the descriptive statistics are or are not consistent with expectations arising from the theoretical literature and past empirical findings.

Beginning with aggregate and per capita equalization payment amounts, we next offer a descriptive overview of regional heterogeneity among the Canadian provinces using several economic indicators. This overview is of interest both to illustrate inequality among the 10 provinces and to examine whether there may be convergence over time, as may be expected if migration is efficient. Third, a description of interprovincial migration and international immigration is offered to address the issue of the mobility of labour in response to differential economic opportunities. Fourth, the per capita revenues and expenditures of provincial governments are provided as evidence of the provincial governments' differing fiscal capacities and the possible relationships of these capacities with migration patterns. The chapter concludes with a brief discussion of ongoing and outstanding issues.

Equalization payments[4] in Canada, 1980–81 to 2015–16

Although per capita equalization payments (see Appendix Table A.2) provide a more accurate understanding of equalization payment in Canada,

---

3 Although equalization payments date back to the 1957–58 period, the text of this chapter and the figures imbedded in it reflect the 1980–81 to 2015–16 period, due to data limitations. For completeness, the Appendix also includes equalization entitlements, the percentage distribution among provinces, and per capita equalization payments back to 1957–58, as well as data for the most recent 2016–17 period.

4 The term, "equalization payments" in this chapter refers to equalization entitlements as calculated by the Department of Finance Canada.

an overview of total equalization payments by destination province is presented in Figure 3.1.[5] In both of the years shown, 1980 and 2015, about half of total payments have gone to Québec (QC). Over the 1980–81 to 2015–16 time period, the smallest percentage going to QC was 38 per cent in 2004–05, and the largest was 60 per cent in 2008–09. However, most years fall into a narrow band of 45–55 per cent. The percentage of total equalization payments going to any province will, of course, reflect not only conditions in that province but also conditions in the other provinces, as well as the size of the province. As other provinces move into or out of the recipient and non-recipient categories, the remaining provinces' proportions are also affected. The low 2004–05 percentage for QC was also the year that Saskatchewan (SK) moved from being a non-recipient province in the preceding year to being a recipient province, capturing 7 per cent of aggregate equalization payments in that year. In 2008–09, when QC received 60 per cent of equalization payments, Newfoundland and Labrador (NL), SK, and British Columbia (BC) had all moved into non-recipient status.

Provinces that have received equalization payments in each of the 36 years represented in these data include Prince Edward Island (PE), Nova Scotia (NS), New Brunswick (NB), QC, and Manitoba (MB), as shown in Appendix Table A.1. NL received equalization payments continually from 1980–81 to 2007–08, but it has been a non-recipient province since then. Alberta (AB) has never received equalization payments over this period, and Ontario had never been a recipient until 2009–10. SK has received payments in 22 of the 36 years under review, and BC in only 7 of the 36 years.

The percentage distribution of payments shown in Figure 3.1 and Appendix Table A.1 are, however, somewhat deceiving because they reflect not just the economic conditions and fiscal capacity of provincial governments but also the population sizes of the provinces. QC, for example, accounts for close to one-quarter of Canada's population, so revenue shortfalls in that province would elicit much larger aggregate payments than they would in a small province such as PE, which has less than one-half of 1 per cent of the national population. Per capita payments, rather than absolute amounts, are thus a more meaningful representation of the amount of equalization payments going to the provinces. Figure 3.2 and Appendix Table A.2 show that the recipients of the highest levels of per

---

5 For more detailed information about the determination of equalization payments, see https://www.fin.gc.ca/fedprov/eqp-eng.asp.

Figure 3.1 Percentage distribution of equalization payments in Canada, 1980–81 and 2015–16

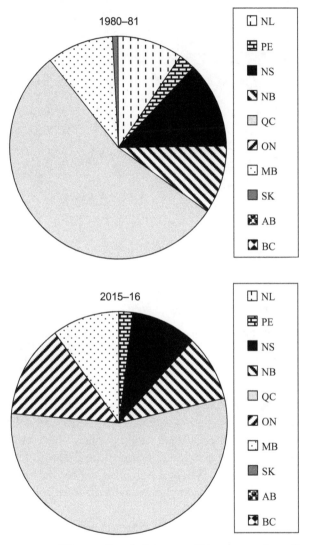

Source: Department of Finance Canada (2015, 2016) by request. An earlier version also appears in Olfert (2016).

capita equalization payments have always been either PE or NL. PE placed first from 1980–81 to 1984–85 and again from 2002–03 to the present. In between, from 1985–86 to 2001–02, NL was the highest per capita recipient. In the most recent year, 2015–16, the per capita equalization

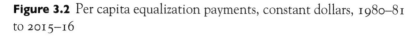

Figure 3.2 Per capita equalization payments, constant dollars, 1980–81 to 2015–16

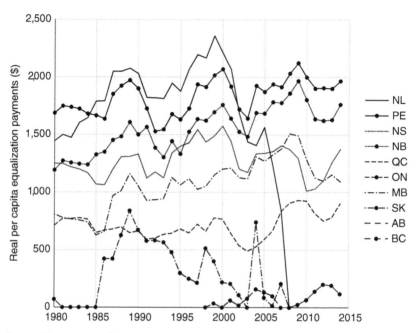

Source: Department of Finance Canada; Statistics Canada CANSIM, *Table: 051–0001 Estimates of Population*. An earlier version also appears in Olfert (2016).

payment was $2,465 in PE, followed by $2,214 in NB, $1,792 in NS, and $1,344 in MB. QC's per capita equalization payments were relatively low at only $1,152. Historically, QC's per capita payments have been less than half those of the highest provincial amounts, and always less than the per capita payments to PE, NB, and NS. Also, except for five early years (1982–83 to 1986–87), QC's per capita payments have been below those of MB.

Only recently a recipient of equalization, ON received very small per capita payments ranging from $27 per capita in 2009–10 to $243 in 2012–13. However, with well over one-third of Canada's population, even those low per capita payments translate into a large budgetary commitment for the federal government, as shown in Figure 3.1. Like ON, BC, when it did receive payments in 7 of the 36 years, was provided small per capita payments, ranging from $17 in 2002–03 to $164 in 2004–05.

Inequalities in provincial economic conditions

The horizontal equity basis for equalization payments may be approximated by several indicators. Gross domestic product (GDP) per capita, the broadest measure of a jurisdiction's economy, varied from \$35,071 (in 2007 dollars) in PE to \$77,680 in AB in the most recent year for which information was available (see Appendix Table A.3). In fact, AB's GDP per capita was more than twice that of PE for every year under review, and it was as high as 2.7 times the PE value in 1980–81. Figure 3.3 shows provincial GDP per capita indexed to the 10-province average in each year.

The positions of the provinces in terms of their relative GDP per capita are remarkably stable over time. AB's per capita GDP is 150 per cent or more of the 10-province average in every year. PE has the lowest per capita GDP in every year, at about 60–70 per cent of the average, with NS and NB just slightly higher. QC's per capita GDP hovers between 82 and 85 per cent

Figure 3.3 Provincial real GDP per capita, indexed to Canada, 1980–81 to 2014–15

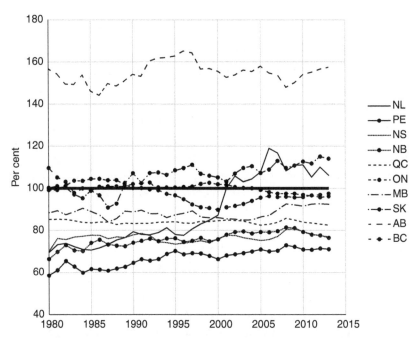

Source: Statistics Canada CANSIM, *Table 384–0038: Gross Domestic Product, Expenditure-Based, Provincial and Territorial, Annual (dollars x 1,000,000); Table 051–0001: Estimates of Population*. An earlier version also appears in Olfert (2016).

of the average. ON strongly influences the national average because of its dominance in the national economy, and its per capita GDP is thus very close to the average, as is BC's.

Two exceptions to this pattern of stability are NL and SK. NL is the major "success story" starting at 70 per cent of the 10-province average and rising to 119 per cent in 2007–08, though falling back to 106 per cent by 2014–15. SK exhibits more modest relative growth over this interval, with per capita GDP at the national average in 1980–81, rising to 114 per cent by 2014–15. Both of these provinces have experienced growth due to high oil prices since about 2000. Both provinces' relative strength was negatively affected by the steep fall in oil prices that began in late 2014.

In spite of this high degree of stability in per capita GDP relative to the national average for provinces other than NL and SK, careful observation suggests very modest convergence over time for PE, NS, NB, and MB. Comparing the 1980–81 and 2013–14 end points, the gap between their per capita GDP levels and the 10-province average is, in most years, closing very slowly over time. This stands in contrast to QC, where there is minor divergence from the average over time, with QC beginning at 85 per cent of the national average in 1981 and falling to 82 per cent in 2014.

Another and perhaps more accurate indicator of economic well-being is household disposable income, that is, income to persons remaining after taxes and including transfers. Disposable income reflects what is actually received as net income by residents, rather than just the value of production, some of which may flow to government and out of the country.[6] Figure 3.4 shows relative per capita household disposable income relationships among the provinces, as was done for the GDP in Figure 3.3. The Canadian average is used as the base to which each of the provinces is indexed to reveal *relative* values over time.

With the exception of AB, there has been considerable convergence over time toward the Canadian average. Excluding AB, the range of indexed values varied from 68 (NL) to 112 (BC) in 1980–81 and decreased to a range between 86 (PE) and 108 (SK) in 2013–14. The equalizing effects of taxes and transfers reduced inequality among provinces overall, although since about 2000, AB diverged sharply from the average driven by the combination of its high GDP per capita and low tax rates. By 2013, AB's indexed per capita household disposable income was 132, or 32 per cent above the national average. In that last year, per capita household disposable income in SK was 8 per cent above the national average.

---

6 Appendix Table A.4 shows household per capita income indexed to the national average.

Figure 3.4 Provincial household disposable income per capita, indexed to Canada, 1980–81 to 2014–15

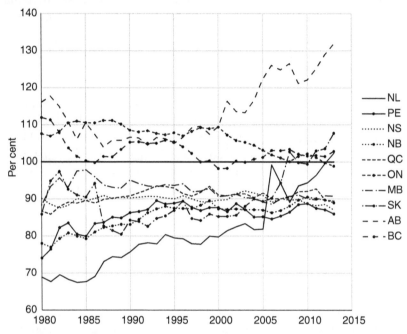

Source: Statistics Canada CANSIM, *Table 384–5000: Data on Long-Run Provincial and Territorial Economic Performance, Annual.* An earlier version also appears in Olfert (2016).

The third major oil producing province, NL has had a somewhat different experience. NL had the lowest per capita disposable income of all the provinces from 1980–81 to 2005–06, ranging from 68 per cent of the national average to 82 per cent, even though its GDP per capita exceeded the national average as early as 2001–02. Only in the last year shown here, 2013–14, did NL's per capita disposable income exceed the national average. Viewed over the entire period, 1980–81 to 2013–14, NL's per capita disposable income increased dramatically from 68 per cent to 102 per cent of the national average. The oil-based economic boom translated into increases in disposable income in NL, SK, and AB, though the levels are somewhat different due to differences in provincial government financial commitments and obligations.

To the extent that relative economic conditions among the provinces translate into differences in provincial government revenues, a substantial degree of horizontal inequity is present, especially in terms of GDP.

Viewed from the perspective of household disposable income, however, this inequity is mostly decreasing. Possible exceptions to the convergence are AB and, since about 1995, QC and the Maritime provinces, where, in both cases, per capita incomes have stabilized at about 90 per cent of the Canadian average.

Migration responses to regional economic differences

Both interprovincial migration and international immigration would be expected to reflect the decisions of individuals to move to locations with higher (real) wages, lower unemployment rates, better weather, and better public services, all else being constant. To the extent that migration does occur in response to economic incentives, migration is efficient and would contribute to the equalizing of employment and incomes among the provinces over time.

Moving to better economic opportunity would be consistent with moving to AB and, more recently, to SK and NL. Based on the economic indicators presented above, we would expect net out-migration from the Atlantic provinces (except NL after 2002), QC, and MB. In the case of QC, the language difference may pose a barrier to mobility not present elsewhere (Bakhshi et al. 2009). If moving to better weather is a factor, then we might see net positive migration to BC even though its economic indicators are very near the national average.

Figure 3.5 and Appendix Table A.5 show the net interprovincial migration per 1,000 inhabitants over our study period. Because of the high volatility and similarity of net interprovincial migration rates, the data are presented in two panels, a and b. Panel 3.5a includes those provinces where we might expect positive net migration rates if migrants flow to better economic opportunities (based on the most recent year). Included are NL, ON, SK, AB, and BC, even though NL's experience is positive relative to the national average only after 2000. This first group represents currently non-recipient provinces in terms of equalization payments, though NL has been a part of this category only since 2008. Panel 3.5b shows those provinces where we would expect more or less consistently negative net interprovincial migration, that is PE, NS, NB, QC, and MB, those provinces with relatively low disposable incomes and also provinces that consistently receive equalization payments.

From Figure 3.5a, it is clear that AB does indeed have positive net interprovincial migration for most of the years since the mid-1990s. However, it is also clear that, during the previous collapse in oil prices (1982–83 to 1988–89) and again during the 2009 recession, net interprovincial

72

Figure 3.5 Interprovincial migration per 1,000 inhabitants, 1980–81 to 2014–15

a. Provinces NL, ON, SK, AB, and BC

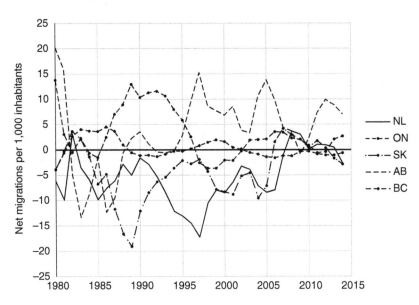

b. Provinces PE, NS, NB, QC, and MB

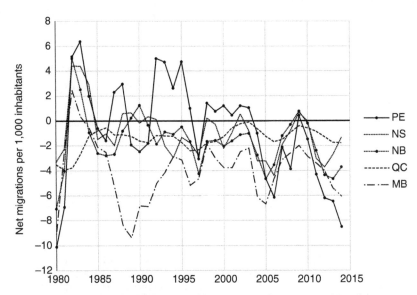

Source: Statistics Canada CANSIM, *Table 051–0004, Components of Population Growth.* An earlier version also appears in Olfert (2016).

migration to AB was negative. Just as booms bring in-migrants on net, the subsequent collapse results in out-migration. Clearly, the relationship between net migration patterns bears a closer positive relationship to per capita disposable income differences than it does to relative GDP per capita. This is as expected because not all of the GDP becomes disposable income. GDP shows the value of production in that jurisdiction, not the incomes received in that province. Owners of capital, for example, may be located in other provinces and countries where they receive their profits and returns to capital. Labour (and population) migration, however, will be more sensitive to after-tax incomes, represented by disposable income.[7]

NL experienced negative out-migration over virtually the entire time period, which is consistent with NL's relative disposable income levels until about 2005. NL's net migration was positive between 2008 and 2013. A similar pattern is seen for SK, where, except for the 2007–12 period, interprovincial net migration has been negative. ON has experienced both positive and negative migration, though overall it is more often positive than negative. The same is true for BC, where high positive net migration rates from 1987 to 1995 were followed by out-migration from 1997 to 2002 before becoming positive again. Though the BC pattern is generally consistent with relative disposable income levels, a milder climate in BC is likely also a factor for in-migration. Based on consideration of relative disposable income alone, the ON net in-migration rate might have been expected to be positive more often.

Turning to the provinces that have generally had relatively poor economic performance, as represented by relative per capita GDP and disposable income levels, most of the net interprovincial migration rates are negative, as expected (see Figure 3.5b). PE has positive rates more often than might be expected. However, the very small population base likely distorts the apparent magnitude of the migration flows. The other consideration is that, in some cases, return migration may be an important factor. There is typically out-migration to areas of better opportunity (AB, for example) during a boom in the destination provinces, but when there is a downturn in the migration destination, return migration occurs. MB has the worst out-migration performance in most years, though it does not have the lowest disposable income levels. QC is consistently negative, though

---

7 The relationship between GDP and disposable income is as follows: GDP – depreciation – indirect taxes – retained earnings – corporate income taxes – personal income taxes + transfers to persons = disposable income. Another way to think about this is that GDP is the total value of production occurring in that jurisdiction, while disposable income is what ultimately becomes the discretionary income of individuals, which can then be either spent or saved.

the out-migration rates are low, likely due to language barriers as well as economic conditions (Coulombe 2006).

As is apparent from these figures, net migration patterns are strongly related to relative disposable income levels, though relative income is certainly not the only determinant. As already discussed, climate may be an important consideration, especially for the population outside the employment cohorts. Return migration and considerations such as the size and complexity of the local economy will also affect migration flows.

In addition to interprovincial migration, the destination of international migration will also reflect the relative economic conditions across provinces. The data show, however, that immigration flows are likely less sensitive to interprovincial differences in GDP or disposable income and more sensitive to the size and diversity of the existing populations. ON had the highest number of immigrants per 1,000 inhabitants for most years up to 2007–08, closely followed by BC (see Appendix Table A.6). AB was usually in third place, though often it was matched, and sometimes surpassed, by QC.

The combination of the recession beginning in 2008 and the high price of oil up until the fall of 2014 modified international immigration patterns during the 2008–14 period. AB and SK matched or exceeded ON and BC during these years. It remains to be seen how lower oil prices since 2015 will affect immigration patterns and other socio-economic indicators. Perhaps most surprising, in light of the economic indicators already discussed, is MB's performance in terms of immigration. From 2008–09 to 2014–15, MB had the highest number of immigrants per 1,000 inhabitants. Deliberate provincial-level immigration policies and programs are likely responsible for this performance.

Provincial government revenues

Canada's equalization program is, of course, focused on the fiscal capacity of the provinces, not on GDP or disposable income differences, though government revenue is certainly related to major economic indicators. Figure 3.6 shows provincial government per capita revenues over the 1980–81 to 2015–16 period for the two groups of provinces shown above, which roughly represent recipient and non-recipient provinces. To the extent that economic conditions, as reflected in GDP per capita, will be positively correlated with government revenues, we would expect relative per capita government revenues to reflect relative per capita GDP patterns closely.

Indexed per capita provincial government revenues (excluding equalization payments) are shown in Figure 3.6 and in Appendix Table A.7. For

Figure 3.6 Per capita provincial government revenue (excluding equalization payments), indexed to the 10-province aggregate level, 1981–82 to 2013–14

a. Provinces NL, ON, SK, AB, and BC

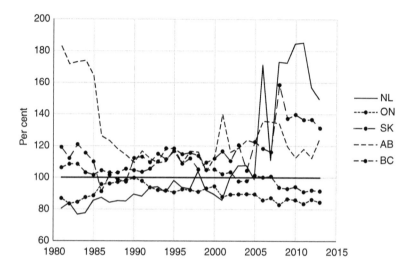

b. Provinces PE, NS, NB, QC, and MB

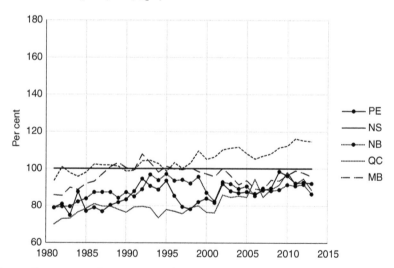

Source: For 1981–88, Statistics Canada CANSIM, *Table 384–0004: Government Sector Revenue and Expenditure, Provincial Economic Accounts, Annual (dollars)*; for 1989–2009, Statistics Canada CANSIM, *Table 385–0002: Federal, Provincial and Territorial General Government Revenue and Expenditures*; and for 2007–13, Statistics Canada CANSIM, *Table 385–0034: Canadian Government Finance Statistics (CGFS)*.

ease of presentation, as with Figure 3.5 showing interprovincial migration, Figure 3.6a includes provinces that have been largely non-recipients (ON, SK, AB, BC, and NL because of its recent ascent to the non-recipient category), and Figure 3.6b shows PE, NS, NB, QC, and MB, the consistently recipient provinces. In all cases, each province's revenue is indexed to the 10-province aggregate. It should be noted that these data depict actual revenues, as per the provincial accounts, not revenue capacity as measured in the equalization formula. The revenues shown here are the result of applying actual provincial tax rates to their tax bases. In the equalization formula, average national tax rates are applied to the provincial tax base to arrive at revenue capacity.

Per capita provincial government revenues in Figure 3.6a show that AB did indeed have per capita revenues above the national average, ranging from 109 to 183 per cent of the national average. NL's recent change in fortune is very evident, though its revenue also exceeded the national average in 2003 and it remained an equalization recipient province until 2008. In 2011, NL's per capita provincial government revenue was 170 per cent that of the national average. Somewhat surprising is that, except for 1986, 1988, and 1989, SK's per capita provincial government revenue exceeded the national average even though this province was a recipient province continuously from 1986 to 2007, except for one of those 22 years. Surprising, in light of its predominantly non-recipient status, ON's per capita provincial government revenue is below the 10-province aggregate in every year shown here, falling to as low as 84 per cent of the national average. BC's per capita provincial government revenue is above the national average in most years, remaining fairly close to the average even when it falls slightly below.

Figure 3.6b shows the per capita provincial government revenues for those provinces that have consistently received equalization payments. For the most part, their per capita revenues are indeed below the national average, with NS being among the lowest, often less than 80 per cent of the national average. Perhaps somewhat surprising is the fact that QC's per capita revenue is above the national average in most years, even though it has always been a recipient province. This circumstance likely reflects the fact that QC has chosen to have a bigger government sector, with higher tax rates, than most of the other provinces. MB's per capita revenue remains close to the national average, though slightly below.

There is clearly some difference between a province's relative position in terms of per capita government revenue and whether it received equalization payments or not. This difference is a reflection of differing tax policies among the provinces, variations in the tax bases that are included in the calculation over time, differences in costs, and formula changes that have occurred over time in terms of the provinces included in the standard of comparison.

Returning to the issue of the feared fiscally induced migration, we can usefully consider whether the provinces with above average economic outcomes are also those that attract interprovincial migrants. This consideration is not by way of identifying cause and effect, as there will be many influences. However, it is useful to examine the descriptive data to see whether the direction of migration is consistent with what we would expect if there were indeed fiscally induced migration. Using per capita government revenue as an imperfect representation of fiscal capacity, there is, with some exceptions, weak support for the case that provinces with relatively high per capita government revenues are more likely to have positive interprovincial migration, and vice versa. For example, AB has both high revenues and mostly positive interprovincial migration. NS, NB, and MB have below average revenues and mostly negative net migration. On the other hand, SK has mostly above average revenues and for the most part uniformly negative net migration; QC has mostly above average revenue and consistently negative net migration. Rigorous empirical analysis, which is beyond the scope of this book, would be required to sort out the underlying cause-effect relationships.

Provincial government per capita expenditures

Although revenue capacity is targeted directly in the equalization formula, the stated purpose of equalization is, of course, to enable provinces to provide roughly equivalent levels of service for their constituents. Though the "level of services" will be difficult to measure and compare, perhaps some impression of this factor can be discerned from the provincial per capita expenditures, again indexed to the national average. It is acknowledged that per capita expenditures are a very crude first approximation; needs and costs of providing services will also be important in assessing the adequacy of the revenues. Nevertheless, they are a useful starting point for further investigation.

Because revenues are not fully "equalized," one might expect a lesser ability to provide services on the part of the recipient provinces than the non-recipient provinces, even though the expenditures observed include the use of equalization payments. If, however, expenditures are higher in non-recipient provinces than in recipient provinces, all else being constant, this would confirm the horizontal inequities that would result in lower costing service provision in the non-recipient provinces (and inefficient migration). On the other hand, if per capita expenditures are higher in recipient provinces, there may be cause to consider the reasons for this, including potential issues such as the flypaper effect or the inefficient use of public funds, though a cause-effect inference would require a rigorous analysis well beyond simple descriptive statistics.

Figure 3.7 and Appendix Table A.8 show per capita provincial government expenditures, again for the same two groups of provinces identified above. Figure 3.7a shows per capita provincial government expenditures for the five provinces that have mostly or recently been non-recipients—NL, ON, SK, AB, and BC—while Figure 3.7b shows per capita expenditures for those provinces that have consistently been recipients of equalization payments—PE, NS, NB, QC, and MB.

The non-recipient provinces might be expected to have higher per capita expenditures, as they are better able to provide services. Figure 3.7a, however, shows that ON has always had per capita expenditures below the national average, ranging from 82 to 96 per cent of the national average. BC has had expenditures below the national levels for 23 of the 33 years, and when these expenditures were above the national average, they were only slightly higher. AB has had higher per capita expenditures for 25 of the 33 years, and SK for 31 years, including the years when SK was a recipient province. NL has always had above average per capita expenditures, more markedly during the latter years when it became a non-recipient. Overall, ON and BC do not exhibit higher than average per capita expenditures, as might be expected if higher revenue capacity was the primary driver. Per capita provincial government expenditure is above average in AB, SK, and NL, including during the years when the latter two provinces were equalization recipients.

The empirical investigation required to establish the reasons for the relative per capita expenditures is well beyond the scope of this book. A rigorous empirical analysis that held all other factors equal, such as economies of size and scale, the cost of providing services in each jurisdiction, and the preferences of the population, would be required to investigate the possible presence of a flypaper effect. The potential negative impact on interprovincial migration, which might indicate a welfare trap, also bears further consideration, but likewise would require a rigorous analysis. Again, the required investigation is well beyond the scope of this book. However, relatively high rates of net out-migration from recipient provinces suggest that people are, in fact, moving to higher employment and income opportunities. Whether the out-migration is muted because of transfers is not clear. With efficient migration in the direction of better economic opportunities, we would expect economic conditions to become more similar across provinces over time. The fact that per capita disposable income is

Figure 3.7 Provincial government per capita expenditures, indexed to the 10-province aggregate level, 1981–82 to 2013–14

a. Provinces NL, ON, SK, AB, and BC

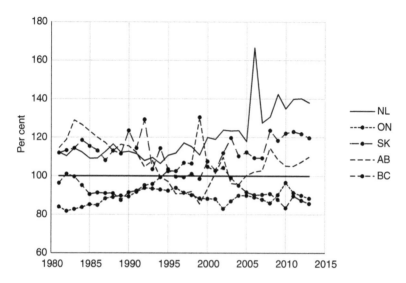

b. Provinces PE, NS, NB, QC, and MB

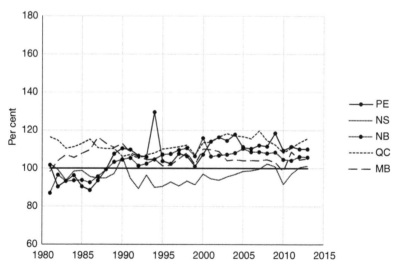

Source: For 1981–88, Statistics Canada CANSIM, *Table 384–0004: Government Sector Revenue and Expenditure, Provincial Economic Accounts, Annual (dollars)*; for 1989–2009, Statistics Canada CANSIM, *Table 385–0002: Federal, Provincial and Territorial General Government Revenue and Expenditures*; and for 2007–13, Statistics Canada CANSIM, *Table 385–0034: Canadian Government Finance Statistics (CGFS)*.

showing some convergence over time is encouraging, though the rate of convergence is slow.

However, interpreting the above expenditure patterns requires consideration of several factors other than economic conditions and revenues, including the sizes of the provinces, both geographically and demographically. Per unit costs of service delivery are undoubtedly higher in large geographic areas with dispersed small populations (e.g., SK). Similarly, a small population, even when it is fairly concentrated, will reduce the ability to realize economies of size and scale in the service facilities as well as in their delivery. In addition, economic booms that drive up labour costs in the private sector will also drive up that component of public expenditures. Some of the per capita expenditure differences are likely the result of differences in the scale and cost of services. In addition, as already noted, a fundamental reason for a federal form of government is to accommodate differences in the preferences of populations across jurisdictions, for example, to accommodate the possibility that residents in some subnational jurisdictions will choose to reside in jurisdictions with larger public sectors.

Outstanding and ongoing issues

Several conceptual as well as practical issues remain unresolved. On the conceptual front, in spite of decades of information about equalization payments and the economic performance of the provinces, it is not clear that fiscally induced migration occurs or, if it does, whether it is serious enough to warrant intervention. Interprovincial migration rates are relatively high and, for the most part, in a direction consistent with movement to higher productivity. Where migration occurs in the direction of greater fiscal capacity, this migration might happen because greater fiscal capacity is correlated with better economic opportunities.

The question of horizontal equity is equally difficult to answer. Clearly, there are inequities in GDP, in disposable income, and in government revenues and expenditures. The fact that there appears to be some convergence in disposable income per capita is encouraging, though this convergence is also partly due to labour mobility in the direction of higher productivity, as well as (possibly) being the effect of government policies such as equalization payments. There is no apparent convergence in per capita provincial government revenues (either before or after equalization) or in per capita expenditures. Concerns that equalization payments might have a flypaper effect or the potential for creating a welfare trap require vigilance and further empirical research.

Historically, virtually all of the changes to the equalization program have been in response to practical budgetary considerations or for political reasons. These practical issues will continue to be important. Although provincial and federal policymakers seem somewhat committed to the 10-province standard, it is currently eclipsed by the federal government's fixed-pool approach; the standard, however, still underlies the calculations. As economic conditions change, especially in relation to oil prices, the 10-province standard could again become the binding constraint. Questions such as which revenue sources to include, to what extent, and whether to use revenue capacity or actual revenue also seem mostly resolved, though, with the recent return to volatility in resource prices, these issues may resurface. When resource prices are low, there is less pressure to remove non-renewable resource revenues because their inclusion is less consequential. The distinction between revenues from renewable (hydro) and non-renewable (oil) natural resources will likely be open to debate from time to time.

The three-year moving average assessment of revenues, installed to provide stability and predictability, is currently being questioned. Although, in principle, the provision of stable and predictable equalization payments has merit, there is a trade-off between this security and the speed with which equalization payments can respond to downturns in the provincial economies, such as those SK and NL faced in 2016. Special cases and ad hoc exceptions have been made in the past for political reasons, and though they cannot be ruled out in the future, there is some resistance to launching more of these.

The overriding driver of change to the equalization program has been, and will likely continue to be, the federal budgetary implications. If Ontario's economy and its revenue sources do not recover relative to the average, its continued inclusion as a recipient province will lead to major changes in the equalization formula simply because of the budgetary impact. However, the gradual recovery of Ontario's manufacturing sector, due, in part, to the lower value of the dollar occasioned by the drop in oil prices may avert this problem; coincidentally, lower oil prices will also result in a lower 10-province standard. Although economic efficiency arguments may underlie the design of the equalization payments program and the empirical investigation of its effects and effectiveness, expediency is likely to continue to be the driver of program design.

References

Arrow, Kenneth J. 1969. "The Organization of Economic Activity: Issues Pertinent to the Choice of Market versus Non-market Allocation." In *The Analysis and Evaluation of Public Expenditures: The PPB-System*, edited by the Joint Economic

Committee, 91st Cong., 1st sess., 1: 47–66. Washington, DC: United States Government Printing Office.

Atkinson, Michael M., Daniel Béland, Gregory P. Marchildon, Kathleen McNutt, Peter W.B. Phillips, and Ken Rasmussen. 2013. *Governance and Public Policy in Canada: A View from the Provinces*. Toronto: University of Toronto Press.

Bakhshi, Samira, Mohammad Shakeri, M. Rose Olfert, Mark D. Partridge, and Simon Weseen. 2009. "Do Local Residents Value Federal Transfers: Evidence from Interprovincial Migration in Canada." *Public Finance Review* 37 (3): 235–68. http://dx.doi.org/10.1177/1091142109331638.

Bergvall, Daniel, Claire Charbit, Dirk-Jan Kraan, and Olaf Merk. 2006. "Intergovernmental Transfers and Decentralised Public Spending." *OECD Journal on Budgeting* 5 (4): 111–58. http://dx.doi.org/10.1787/budget-v5-art24-en.

Besley, Timothy, and Stephen Coate. 2003. "Centralized versus Decentralized Provision of Local Public Goods: A Political Economy Approach." *Journal of Public Economics* 87 (12): 2611–37. http://dx.doi.org/10.1016/S0047-2727(02)00141-X.

Bird, Richard M., and Andrey V. Tarasov. 2004. "Closing the Gap: Fiscal Imbalances and Intergovernmental Transfers in Developed Federations." *Environment and Planning C: Government and Policy* 22 (1): 77–102. http://dx.doi.org/10.1068/c0328.

Boadway, Robin. 2004. "The Theory and Practice of Equalization." *CESifo Economic Studies* 50 (1): 211–54. http://dx.doi.org/10.1093/cesifo/50.1.211.

Boadway, Robin. 2012. "International Lessons in Fiscal Federalism Design." *eJournal of Tax Research* 10 (1): 21–48. https://www.business.unsw.edu.au/research-site/publications-site/ejournaloftaxresearch-site/Documents/paper3_v1on1_Boadway.pdf.

Boadway, Robin, and Frank Flatters. 1982a. "Efficiency and Equalization Payments in a Federal System of Government: A Synthesis and Extension of Recent Results." *Canadian Journal of Economics / Revue canadienne d'Economique* 15 (4): 613–33. http://dx.doi.org/10.2307/134918.

Boadway, Robin, and Frank Flatters. 1982b. *Equalization in a Federal State: An Economic Analysis*. Ottawa: Economic Council of Canada.

Bolton, Roger. 1992. "'Place Prosperity vs. People Prosperity' Revisited: An Old Issue with a New Angle." *Urban Studies* 29 (2): 185–203. http://dx.doi.org/10.1080/00420989220080261.

Bradford, David F., and Wallace E. Oates. 1971. "Towards a Predictive Theory of Intergovernmental Grants." *American Economic Review* 61 (2): 440–48.

Brennan, Geoffrey, and James M. Buchanan. 1980. *The Power to Tax: Analytical Foundations of a Fiscal Constitution*. Cambridge: Cambridge University Press.

Buchanan, James M. 1950. "Federalism and Fiscal Equity." *American Economic Review* 40 (4): 583–99.

Bucovetsky, Sam. 1998. "Federalism, Equalization and Risk Aversion." *Journal of Public Economics* 67 (3): 301–28.

Coulombe, Serge. 2006. "Internal Migration, Asymmetric Shocks, and Interprovincial Economics Adjustments in Canada." *International Regional Science Review* 29 (2): 199–223. http://dx.doi.org/10.1177/0160017606286357.

Courchene, Thomas J. 1970. "Interprovincial Migration and Economic Adjustment." *Canadian Journal of Economics / Revue canadienne d'Economique* 3 (4): 550–76. http://dx.doi.org/10.2307/133598.

Courchene, Thomas J. 1984. "The Political Economy of Canadian Constitution-Making: The Canadian Economic-Union Issue." *Public Choice* 44 (1): 201–49. http://dx.doi.org/10.1007/BF00124824.

Courchene, Thomas J. 2005. *Resource Revenues and Equalization: Five-Province vs. National-Average Standards, Alternatives to the Representative Tax System, and Revenue-Sharing Pools*. Working Paper No. 2005–04. Montréal: Institute for Research on Public Policy.

Crowley, Brian Lee, and Bobby O'Keefe. 2006a. *Why Some Provinces Are More Equal Than Others*. AIMS Special Equalization Commentary Series No. 1. Halifax: Atlantic Institute for Market Studies. http://www.aims.ca/site/media/aims/Equalization1.pdf.

Crowley, Brian Lee, and Bobby O'Keefe. 2006b. *The Flypaper Effect*. AIMS Special Equalization Commentary Series No. 2. Halifax: Atlantic Institute for Market Studies. http://aims.wpengine.com/site/media/aims/Equalization2.pdf.

Dahlby, Bev. 2002. "The Incentive Effects of Fiscal Equalization Grants." Paper presented at the AIMS/MEI/FCPP conference, Equalization: Welfare Trap or Helping Hand? Montréal, Quebec, October 25. http://www.iedm.org/files/011025dahlbypaper.pdf.

Dahlby, Bev. 2005. "Review of the Canadian Equalization and Territorial Funding System." Paper prepared for the Expert Panel on Equalization and Territorial Formula Financing. http://citeseerx.ist.psu.edu/viewdoc/download?doi=10.1.1.500.5208&rep=rep1&type=pdf.

Dahlby, Bev. 2011. "The Marginal Cost of Public Funds and the Flypaper Effect." *International Tax and Public Finance* 18 (3): 304–21. http://dx.doi.org/10.1007/s10797-010-9160-x.

Dahlby, Bev, and Ergete Ferede. 2016. "The Stimulative Effects of Intergovernmental Grants and the Marginal Cost of Public Funds." *International Tax and Public Finance* 23 (1): 114–39. http://dx.doi.org/10.1007/s10797-015-9352-5.

Day, Kathleen M. 1992. "Interprovincial Migration and Local Public Goods." *Canadian Journal of Economics / Revue canadienne d'Economique* 25 (1): 123–44. http://dx.doi.org/10.2307/135714.

Day, Kathleen M., and Stanley L. Winer. 2006. "Policy-Induced Internal Migration: An Empirical Investigation of the Canadian Case." *International Tax and Public Finance* 13 (5): 535–64. http://dx.doi.org/10.1007/s10797-006-6038-z.

Department of Finance Canada. 2015. *Federal Support to Provinces and Territories*. Retrieved October 2015 from http://www.fin.gc.ca/fedprov/mtp-eng.asp.

Department of Finance Canada. 2016. *Federal Support to the Provinces and Territories*. Retrieved December 2016 from https://www.fin.gc.ca/fedprov/mtp-eng.asp.

Ferede, Ergete. 2014. *The Incentive Effects of Equalization Grants on Fiscal Policy*. SPP Research Papers No. 7 (23). Alberta: The School of Public Policy, University of Calgary. https://www.policyschool.ca/wp-content/uploads/2016/03/ferede-equalization.pdf.

Flatters, Frank, Vernon Henderson, and Peter Mieszkowski. 1974. "Public Goods, Efficiency, and Regional Fiscal Equalization." *Journal of Public Economics* 3 (2): 99–112. http://dx.doi.org/10.1016/0047-2727(74)90028-0.

Glaeser, Edward L., Jed Kolko, and Albert Saiz. 2001. "Consumer City." *Journal of Economic Geography* 1 (1): 27–50. http://dx.doi.org/10.1093/jeg/1.1.27.

Gramlich, Edward M. 1977. "Intergovernmental Grants: A Review of the Empirical Literature." In *The Political Economy of Fiscal Federalism*, edited by Wallace Oates, 219–39. Lexington: D.C. Heath.

Grossman, Philip J. 1990. "The Impact of Federal and State Grants on Local Government Spending: A Test of the Fiscal Illusion Hypothesis." *Public Finance Quarterly* 18 (3): 313–27. http://dx.doi.org/10.1177/109114219001800304.

Hall, Jeremy L. 2008. "The Changing Federal Grant Structure and Its Potential Effects on State and Local Community Development Efforts." *Journal of Public Budgeting, Accounting and Financial Management* 20 (1): 46–71.

Hamilton, Jonathan H. 1986. "The Flypaper Effect and the Deadweight Loss from Taxation." *Journal of Urban Economics* 19 (2): 148–55. http://dx.doi.org/10.1016/0094-1190(86)90036-7.

Hamlin, Alan P. 1991. "Decentralization, Competition and the Efficiency of Federalism." *Economic Record* 67 (3): 193–204. http://dx.doi.org/10.1111/j.1475-4932.1991.tb02546.x.

Hercowitz, Zvi, and David Pines. 1991. "Migration with Fiscal Externalities." *Journal of Public Economics* 46 (2): 163–80. http://dx.doi.org/10.1016/0047-2727(91)90002-J.

Hines, James R., Jr., and Richard H. Thaler. 1995. "Anomalies: The Flypaper Effect." *Journal of Economic Perspectives* 9 (4): 217–26. http://www.jstor.org/stable/2138399.

Inman, Robert P. 2008. *The Flypaper Effect.* National Bureau of Economic Research Working Paper 14579. Cambridge, MA: National Bureau of Economic Research. http://dx.doi.org/10.3386/w14579.

Kneebone, Ronald D. 2012. *How You Pay Determines What You Get: Alternative Financing Options as a Determinant of Publicly Funded Health Care in Canada.* SPP Research Paper No. 12 (21). Alberta: The School of Public Policy, University of Calgary. http://dx.doi.org/10.2139/ssrn.2099844.

Logan, Robert R. 1986. "Fiscal Illusion and the Grantor Government." *Journal of Political Economy* 94 (6): 1304–18. http://dx.doi.org/10.1086/261434.

Martinez-Vazquez, Jorge, and Jameson Boex. 2001. *The Design of Equalization Grants: Theory and Applications.* Washington, DC: World Bank. https://www.researchgate.net/publication/265142703_The_design_of_equalization_grants_Theory_and_applications.

Mieszkowski, Peter M., and Eric Toder. 1983. "Taxation of Energy Resources." In *Fiscal Federalism and the Taxation of Natural Resources,* edited by Charles E. McLure and Peter M. Mieszkowski, 65–91. Northampton, MA: Lexington Books.

Musgrave, Richard A. 1959. *The Theory of Public Finance.* New York: McGraw-Hill.

Myers, Gordon M. 1990. "Optimality, Free Mobility, and Regional Authority in a Federation." *Journal of Public Economics* 43 (1): 107–21. http://dx.doi.org/10.1016/0047-2727(90)90053-K.

Oates, Wallace E. 1972. *Fiscal Federalism.* New York: Harcourt Brace Janovich.

Oates, Wallace E. 2005. "Toward a Second-Generation Theory of Fiscal Federalism." *International Tax and Public Finance* 12 (4): 349–73. http://dx.doi.org/10.1007/s10797-005-1619-9.

Olfert, M. Rose. 2016. "Regional Inequality and Decentralized Governance: Canada's Provinces." *Review of Regional Studies* 46 (3): 201–22.

Olfert, M. Rose, Mark D. Partridge, Julio Berdegué, Javier Escobal, Benjamin Jara, and Felis Modrego. 2014. "Places for Place-Based Policy." *Development Policy Review* 32 (1): 5–32. http://dx.doi.org/10.1111/dpr.12041.

Partridge, Mark D., and Dan S. Rickman. 2008. "Place-Based Policy and Rural Poverty: Insights from the Urban Spatial Mismatch Literature." *Cambridge Journal of Regions, Economy and Society* 1 (1): 131–56. http://dx.doi.org/10.1093/cjres/rsm005.

Polèse, Mario, and Richard Shearmur. 2006. "Why Some Regions Will Decline: A Canadian Case Study with Thoughts on Local Development Strategies." *Papers in Regional Science* 85 (1): 23–46. http://dx.doi.org/10.1111/j.1435-5957.2006.00024.x.

Qian, Yingyi, and Gérard Roland. 1998. "Federalism and the Soft Budget Constraint." *American Economic Review* 88 (5): 1143–62.

Rosen, Harvey S., Jean-François Wen, and Tracy Snoddon. 2012. *Public Finance in Canada*. 4th ed. Whitby, ON: McGraw-Hill Ryerson.

Samuelson, Paul A. 1954. "The Pure Theory of Public Expenditure." *Review of Economics and Statistics* 36 (4): 387–89. http://dx.doi.org/10.2307/1925895.

Samuelson, Paul A. 1955. "Diagrammatic Exposition of a Theory of Public Expenditure." *Review of Economics and Statistics* 37 (4): 350–56. http://dx.doi.org/10.2307/1925849.

Shah, Anwar. 1997. *Fiscal Federalism and Macroeconomic Governance: For Better or for Worse?* World Bank Working Paper No. 2005. Washington, DC: World Bank. http://dx.doi.org/10.1596/1813-9450-2005.

Shaw, R. Paul. 1986. "Fiscal versus Traditional Market Variables in Canadian Migration." *Journal of Political Economy* 94 (3, Part 1): 648–66. http://dx.doi.org/10.1086/261394.

Tarroux, Benoît. 2012. "Are Equalization Payments Making Canadians Better Off? A Two-Dimensional Dominance Answer." *Journal of Economic Inequality* 10 (1): 19–44. http://dx.doi.org/10.1007/s10888-010-9152-1.

Tiebout, Charles M. 1956. "A Pure Theory of Local Expenditures." *Journal of Political Economy* 64 (5): 416–24. http://dx.doi.org/10.1086/257839.

Turnbull, Geoffrey K. 1998. "The Overspending and Flypaper Effects of Fiscal Illusion: Theory and Empirical Evidence." *Journal of Urban Economics* 44 (1): 1–26. http://dx.doi.org/10.1006/juec.1997.2056.

Vaillancourt, Francois, and Richard M. Bird. 2004. *Expenditure-Based Equalization Transfers*. International Studies Working Paper 04–10. Atlanta: Andrew Young School of Public Policy, Georgia State University.

Vo, Duc Hong. 2010. "The Economics of Fiscal Decentralization." *Journal of Economic Surveys* 24 (4): 657–79. http://dx.doi.org/10.1111/j.1467-6419.2009.00600.x.

Watson, William G. 1986. "An Estimate of the Welfare Gains from Fiscal Equalization." *Canadian Journal of Economics / Revue canadienne d'Economique* 19 (2): 298–08. http://dx.doi.org/10.2307/135286.

Wilson, L. S. 2003. "Equalization, Efficiency and Migration: Watson Revisited." *Canadian Public Policy* 29 (4): 385–96. http://dx.doi.org/10.2307/3552177.

Winer, Stanley L. 1983. "Some Evidence on the Effect of the Separation of Spending and Taxing Decisions." *Journal of Political Economy* 91 (1): 126–40. http://dx.doi.org/10.1086/261131.

Winer, Stanley L., and Denis Gauthier. 1982. *Internal Migration and Fiscal Structure: An Econometric Study of the Determinants of Interprovincial Migration in Canada*. Ottawa: Economic Council of Canada.

Winer, Stanley L., and Walter Hettich. 2010. "Vertical Imbalance in the Canadian Federation." Paper available from School of Public Policy, Carleton University, Ottawa. http://http-server.carleton.ca/~winers/papers/VFI-Revised-July2-10.pdf.

four

Equalization and the Federal Transfer System

Introduction

This chapter starts with a simple premise, that the major transfers provided by the federal government to the provincial governments in Canada should be seen as a system.[1] This poses a challenge because the study of equalization policy is segregated from the literature on the two specific-purpose transfers for health, postsecondary education, and social assistance and services: currently the Canada Health Transfer (CHT) and the Canada Social Transfer (CST). It is generally perceived that the equalization program redistributes tax revenues between provinces while the CHT and CST ensure minimum national standards in health care and social services. However, from a provincial perspective, because all federal transfers flow into the general revenue funds of the receiving governments, any change causing an increase or decrease in any one transfer has a direct impact on the receiving government's ability to fund expenditures across all areas, including the social policy areas targeted in the specific-purpose transfers.

Another reason for considering the CHT and CST along with equalization is that there was a horizontal redistribution component in the allocation of the CHT and CST, particularly before the two transfers were changed to an equal per capita cash allocation in 2014 and 2007, respectively. Technically speaking, all federal transfers involve a horizontal redistribution of revenue among provinces because these transfers are not allocated based on the source of these revenues. Federal transfers are funded from uniform federal tax efforts across the country rather than from unequal tax efforts in different provinces (these efforts are unequal because of varying provincial fiscal capacities and tax rates). After federal tax revenues from the provinces are pooled in the central treasury, the allocation of federal transfers is mainly based on the population in each province, implying wealthier provinces are contributing more than what they receive

---

1 The territorial governments and the Territorial Formula Financing federal transfer are not discussed in this chapter.

on a per capita basis. In this sense, even equal per capita transfers (such as the CHT and CST) are still redistributing revenue across provinces. Removing what is known as "associated equalization" from the CHT and CST while leaving the equalization program unchanged means that the extent of redistribution through the transfers is reduced, making it more difficult for less wealthy provinces to provide roughly comparable health and social services. Taking the three major federal transfers together as a system allows for a broader perspective and offers more policy options to address the current challenge.

Equalization, the CHT, and the CST constitute the three major federal transfers to provincial governments. Although the equalization program is not the largest transfer (see Figure 4.1)—this claim to fame belongs to the CHT—it is the best known transfer because of its longer history and its constitutional status. For 2015–16, the three transfers combined were budgeted at $63.7 billion, with $34.03 billion earmarked for the CHT, $17.34 billion for equalization and $12.96 billion for the CST. When added together, this transfer system constitutes the single largest expenditure program by the Government of Canada. The only other federal expenditures in the same league are direct transfers to individuals, such as Old Age Security ($46.1 billion) and Employment Insurance ($18.2 billion). In contrast, the federal government is budgeted to spend $18.9 billion on national defence, one of the federal government's single largest direct program expenditures (Treasury Board of Canada 2016). Figure 4.1 also shows that, since its creation in 2004, the CHT has grown faster than both the CST and the equalization program.

At the same time, and by its very nature, the equalization program has had considerably greater variability in terms of its fiscal impact on some

Figure 4.1 Major federal transfers to provinces (millions of dollars), 2015–16.

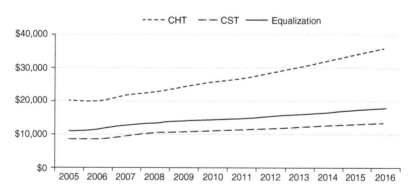

Source: Department of Finance Canada (2015).

Figure 4.2 Major federal transfers (in dollars per capita), 2015–16

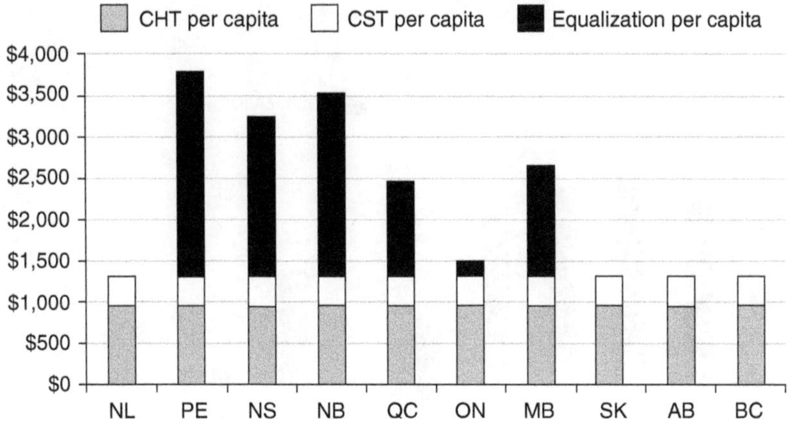

Source: Department of Finance Canada (2015).

consistently equalization-receiving provinces. Figure 4.2 shows the per capita amount of specific-purpose transfer programs (the CHT and CST) and the equalization program in the fiscal year 2015–16.

Since the equalization program was introduced, it has been a much more important source of revenue for the Atlantic provinces than the specific-purpose transfers have been.[2] For example, in 1981, federal transfers constituted almost 40 per cent of the total revenue of the government of New Brunswick and the majority of this revenue consisted of payments from the equalization program. As Figure 4.3a illustrates, New Brunswick's position is similar to that of the other three Atlantic provinces in that year. The situation is the reverse for wealthier provinces (e.g., Ontario and Alberta), which have rarely received payments from the equalization program. In these jurisdictions, the size of CHT and CST contributions is the key factor. As shown in Figure 4.3b, except for newly resource-rich provinces, such as Newfoundland and Labrador this situation has remained remarkably consistent over time, even as transfers as a whole have declined slightly relative to provincial own-source revenues.

---

2 When we assessed the impacts of federal transfer payments on provincial revenues and expenses, we used data from the provincial economic accounts (see Figures 4.3a, 4.3b, 4.7, and 4.8). Provincial economic accounts are complied on a public accounts basis. The transfer amounts in provincial economic accounts are slightly different from the transfer entitlements calculated by the Department of Finance, which are used in Chapter 3. This Equalization data excludes the extra "stabilization" amounts transferred to ON, AB, and BC (see Marshall 2006 for a detailed explanation).

Figure 4.3 Major federal transfer payments, as percentage share of provincial total revenue, 1981 and 2009

a. 1981

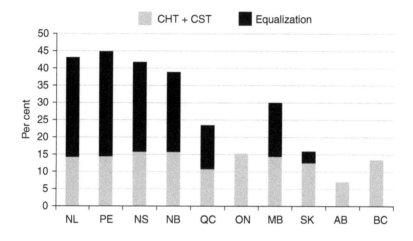

b. 2009

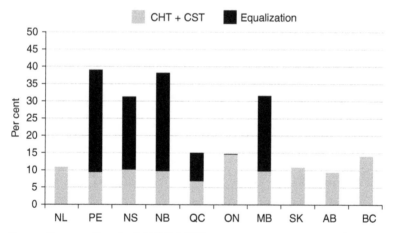

Source: Statistics Canada CANSIM, *Table 384–0011: Intergovernmental Transfers* and *Table 384–0004: Government Sector Revenue and Expenditure, Provincial Economic Accounts.*

These changes suggest that the federal equalization program is of different relative importance to the finance of different provinces. However, what really matters to any individual provincial government is the total cash it receives from all three federal transfers. Given the contested nature and history of the equalization program in Canada, there is room for the federal government to better coordinate the design of the three federal transfers to achieve their policy objectives.

In this chapter, we will first compare the purpose of the equalization program with the aims of specific-purpose transfers. Doing so will allow us to assess the performance of the three transfers as a group in achieving their objectives since the late 1970s. We will then discuss the advantages and disadvantages of using the CHT and CST to achieve, in part, the purpose of horizontal fiscal redistribution and compare this policy with the alternative of further refining the equalization program. In addition, we will consider how each option addresses the different expenditure needs of the provinces.

The objectives of the equalization program and of specific-purpose transfers

This book makes it clear that the fundamental purpose of the equalization program is to promote horizontal fiscal balance among the provinces in the Canadian federation—to improve the equity in distribution of fiscal resources across the 10 provinces. In theory, fiscal resources can be adjusted to capture both the difference in revenue bases among the provinces and the difference in expenditure needs (MacNevin 2004).

However, the current equalization program faces major challenges in ensuring that all provincial governments can deliver reasonably comparative services at reasonably comparative levels of taxation. Payments from the equalization program are currently capped, which has caused a relative decline in the amount of federal money available to the provinces through the program relative to provincial own-source revenues. In 2014, transfers from the equalization program amounted to less than 5 per cent of the total revenues of provincial governments. The formula itself poses a challenge in that, though the program equalizes *up* the fiscal capacity of the less well-off provinces to the national average, it does not equalize *down* the fiscal capacity of the better-off provinces. Finally, in contrast to what is done systematically or ad hoc in other federal countries such as Australia (Chapter 1), equalization in Canada focuses entirely on the revenue capacity of the provinces, ignoring the differences in expenditure needs among the provinces.

This last limitation is entirely defensible if federal transfers—both the equalization program and the specific-purpose transfers—are seen as part of a system rather than in isolation from each other. Historically, the purpose of the transfers has been to serve national objectives through the introduction and maintenance of provincial health, social, and education programs that, together, form what is known as the welfare state. When these programs were first introduced, their cost exceeded the revenue capacities of less wealthy provinces, even after transfers from the equalization program. As a consequence, it was necessary for the federal government to either transfer cash or cede tax room and authority to the provinces to encourage them to assume these new responsibilities and comply with the national standards that went with them.

In this sense, Canada is no different from any other federation where the taxation capacity of the central government is greater than its spending responsibility and the converse holds for sub-national entities. In fact, every federation has a vertical fiscal gap between the central government and its sub-national jurisdictions (Watts 1999). The difference is made up in transfers from the central government to sub-state entities as part of an effort to encourage greater cohesion and establish national standards. The only surprise is the extent to which Canadian provinces are less dependent on central government transfers than sub-national entities in all other OECD federations (Atkinson et al. 2013, 12; Watts 2008). Nonetheless, as a whole, the federal transfer system has played a critical role in accelerating the provision of universal health coverage and social assistance and in increasing access to postsecondary education in less well-off provinces (Boychuk and Banting 2008).

The other important dimension is the conditionality of the CHT and the CST, whose purpose is to ensure a minimum standard for health care and social services (MacNevin 2004; Marchildon and Mou 2014). Although this degree of conditionality appears to be less than the national social policy standards and conditions imposed by central governments in other federations (Requejo 2010; Watts 1999), it has nonetheless served a critical function, particularly in the case of making Medicare a pan-Canadian program (Marchildon 2014; Taylor 1987).

Though the basic idea of an equalization program is embedded in the Constitution, this is not the case for the CHT and CST. However, it is possible to view, at least in principle, the CHT and CST as a constitutional responsibility of the federal government based on Section 36(1) of the 1982 Constitution Act:

(1) Without altering the legislative authority of Parliament or of the provincial legislatures, or the rights of any of them with respect to the exercise of their legislative authority, Parliament and the legislatures, together with the government of Canada and the provincial governments, are committed to
   (a) promoting equal opportunities for the well-being of Canadians;
   (b) furthering economic development to reduce disparity in opportunities; and

    (c) providing essential public services of reasonable quality to all Canadians.

Although there has been limited judicial interpretation of Section 36(1), on its face, the section would appear to provide some constitutional justification for the role of the federal government in upholding, through the CHT, some broad-based pan-Canadian principles such as the five criteria of the Canada Health Act of 1984 (Boadway 2004). At a minimum, these pan-Canadian criteria encourage some sense of shared social citizenship. More ambitiously, these criteria, and the federal transfer funding associated with them, allow lower-income provinces to provide core public services roughly equivalent to those offered by wealthier provinces—a purpose similar to that of the equalization program.

Next, we review the major changes to the conditional health and social transfers enacted since the 1950s, while assessing their impact on the objectives of federal transfers as a system, including the overall effect of federal transfers on the vertical fiscal gap and the distributional impact of the allocation formulas for federal transfers as a group.

Review of the major changes to specific-purpose transfers and their aggregate impacts

In the 1950s and 1960s, the federal government offered cost-sharing grants to provincial and territorial governments to encourage the creation of provincial health and social programs across the country. This began with the Hospital Insurance and Diagnostic Services Act of 1957. This federal law guaranteed all provincial governments 50–50 cost sharing if they adopted universal hospital coverage under a set of national standards reinforced through bilateral federal-provincial agreements. Actual implementation of the act did not begin until 1 July 1958; it would take until 1 January 1961 before all provincial governments had set up programs that met the required national standards (Boychuk 1999; Taylor 1987).

The next step in the development of health transfers in Canada was the federal Medical Care Act of 1966, which similarly offered federal cost-sharing to all provincial governments that agreed to extend universal coverage to physician services under the four principles (public administration, comprehensiveness, universality, and portability) enunciated in the act. Again, provincial implementation was staggered, and it would take until 1 January 1971 before all ten provincial governments had eligible programs (Marchildon and O'Byrne 2013; Taylor 1987).

Introduced by the federal government in 1966, the Canada Assistance Plan (CAP) replaced four pre-existing shared-cost programs, which provided old age assistance, unemployment assistance, and allowances for both blind persons and disabled persons, with a more open-ended shared-cost program for the needy poor. CAP offered cost sharing for eligible provincial social assistance expenditures that met two national standards: eligibility must be based on the need of the recipient rather than on a means test, and no government could impose a residency requirement as a condition for eligibility (Boadway and Hobson 1993; Gauthier 2012).

In 1967, the federal government used the Federal-Provincial Fiscal Arrangements Act enacted that year to introduce general payments—either cost sharing or specific per capita, depending on the preferences of the individual provincial government—for postsecondary education (Gauthier 2012). This payment replaced previous conditional per capita grants offered directly to universities on an annual basis (Boadway and Hobson 1993). The exception was Québec (QC), which, for constitutional reasons, forbade its universities from accepting the grants and, instead, was ceded additional tax room so it could provide its own grants directly to universities (Kitchen and Auld 1995).

In 1977, the cost-sharing grants for health care and postsecondary education were converted to a block transfer called Established Programs Financing (EPF). As illustrated in Figure 4.4, CAP was kept intact as a separate program. Federal and provincial governments agreed to a block transfer made up of roughly equal parts of a cash and tax-point transfer. The increase in cash was indexed to growth in the Canadian economy, while the tax points (13.5 per cent of federal personal income tax and 1 per cent of federal corporate income tax) would generate provincial revenue growth in line with the tax room actually taken up by the respective province and its economic growth. The total EPF payment was allocated on an equal per capita basis. Compared with the cost-sharing program, the block transfer approach was considered to be balanced at the time, in the sense that wealthier provinces would be able to take greater advantage of their tax point transfer while receiving less cash transfer than poorer provinces on a per capita basis.

The EPF block transfer was intended to offer provincial governments greater flexibility in terms of how they managed their social programming. However, in the case of Medicare, this flexibility, combined with the migration of control of funding from the federal health ministry to the federal finance ministry, made it more difficult to enforce national standards. As a consequence, some provincial governments permitted some hospitals and physicians to increase existing fees or impose new direct

Figure 4.4 History of health and social transfers, 1957–2015

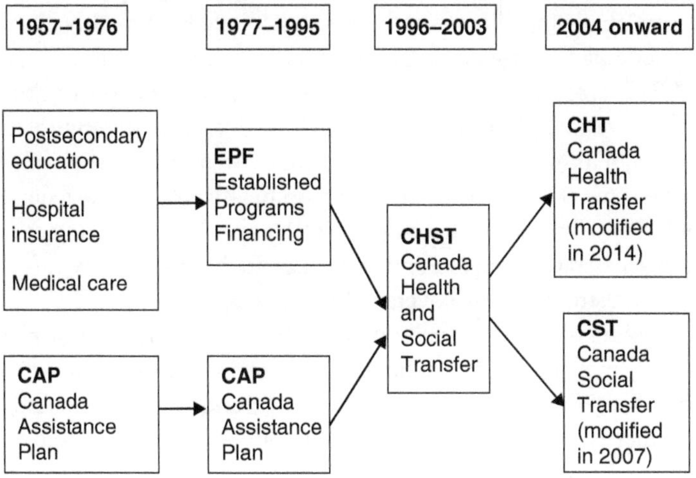

1957–1976	1977–1995	1996–2003	2004 onward

Postsecondary education

Hospital insurance

Medical care

→ EPF Established Programs Financing

→ CHST Canada Health and Social Transfer

→ CHT Canada Health Transfer (modified in 2014)

→ CST Canada Social Transfer (modified in 2007)

CAP Canada Assistance Plan

→ CAP Canada Assistance Plan

Source: Authors' compilation based on Department of Finance Canada (2014).

charges to patients, thereby creating barriers to access. In response, in 1984, the federal government enacted the Canada Health Act. The new legislation replaced the Hospital Insurance and Diagnostic Services Act and the Medical Care Act and introduced a fifth condition on accessibility that discouraged—through reductions in cash transfers—the practice of user fees and extra billing (Marchildon 2014; Taylor 1987).

In 1995, the EPF and CAP were combined in a block grant called the Canada Health and Social Transfer (CHST). Following the practice of the EPF, the CHST also included a tax point transfer and a cash transfer, and the total CHST was allocated on an equal per capita basis. This change was accompanied by a major overall cut in the level of cash transfers to the provinces, precipitating years of federal-provincial conflict. In 2002, the Royal Commission on the Future of Health Care in Canada, popularly known as the Romanow Commission, called for a restoration of federal funding, along with more vigilant monitoring, enforcement, and expansion of national standards. To improve transparency and accountability, the Romanow Commission also recommended the splitting of the block transfer into separate health and social transfers (Romanow 2002).

Following a First Ministers' Accord on Health Care Renewal in 2003, the federal government divided the CHST into the CHT and the CST on 1 April 2004 (McIntosh 2004). On 16 September 2004, following an intense period of intergovernmental negotiations, *A 10-Year Plan to Strengthen Health Care* was produced (CICS 2004). In response to years of complaints about insufficient and unpredictable federal health care transfers, the federal government committed itself to increase the cash portion of the CHT program by 6 per cent annually from 2006–07 to 2013–14. This change restored longer-term (7 years) predictability in terms of annual increases, albeit at a level costly to the federal treasury. At the same time, to achieve some pan-Canadian direction on health reform, the federal government created a temporary (five-year) Health Reform Transfer of $16 billion to accelerate changes in priority areas, including primary care, home care, and catastrophic drug coverage (Fard 2009).

Although it received virtually no attention when the 10-year plan was announced, an element of "associated equalization" was built into the CHT and CST, a carryover from the predecessor EPF and CHST. Both CHT and CST payments included a tax point component and a cash component, and the total transfer was allocated on an equal per capita basis. Figure 4.5 shows the total size of these transfer payments from 1981 to 2013, the longest time period for which we could find comparable data about the size of federal transfer payments.

As illustrated in Figure 4.5, conditional grants as a group have become more significant relative to the equalization program, a trend that has

Figure 4.5 Size of major federal cash transfer payments to provinces (millions of dollars), 1981–2013

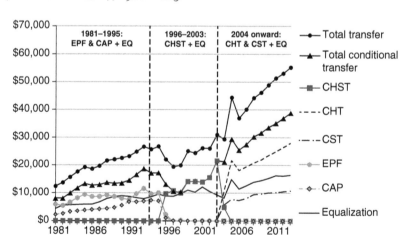

Note: In this figure, "EQ" means the equalization program payment.
Source: Statistics Canada CANSIM, *Table 380–0080: Revenue, Expenditure and Budgetary Balance—General Governments* (current dollars).

been pronounced since 2004. This trend is primarily due to the 6 per cent annual escalator in the CHT as a result of the 10-year plan. In contrast, the equalization program has exhibited a steady but much slower growth since 1981. By 2013, CHT and CST payments combined were more than double the size of the equalization program payment. This review of the history and growth of the three major transfers suggests that, although equalization is often the centre of policy debate, health and social transfers have become a more important source of revenue for provincial governments over time, and are therefore deserving of greater scholarly focus than in the past.

Until recently, there were horizontal redistribution components in the allocation formulas for the CHT and CST—a form of "associated equalization" at the margins. However, adoption of the equal per capita cash transfer allocation for the CST in 2007 and for the CHT in 2014 removed such redistribution (Marchildon and Mou 2014). As a result, to finance rapidly growing social and health expenditures, less well-off provinces have to rely more heavily on payments from the equalization program to supplement own-source revenues.

Next, we evaluate the aggregate impacts of the three transfers as a group, in terms of their two main policy objectives: to reduce the vertical fiscal gap between the federal government and the provincial governments and to ensure provinces provide reasonably comparable public services at reasonably comparable tax rates.

The aggregate impact of the federal transfers in reducing the vertical fiscal gap

Transfer from the central government to sub-state governments is the most common method of reducing the vertical fiscal gap in a federation. In this regard, federal transfers aim to augment the fiscal capacity of sub-state governments and help them better afford public services. The question of degree remains. In particular, to what extent has this system of transfers helped sub-state governments finance public services? Figure 4.6 shows the percentage share of the total amount of these transfer payments in the total program expenses of provincial and territorial governments.

Figure 4.6 reveals rather contrasting patterns. While the total program expenses of provincial and territorial governments quadrupled between 1981 and 2013, the contribution of federal cash transfer payments to these program expenses declined in relative terms, making up 19 per cent of program expenses in 1981 and declining to roughly 14 per cent between 2006 and 2013.

Figure 4.6 Federal cash transfer payments, as a percentage share of provincial and territorial program expenses, 1981–2013

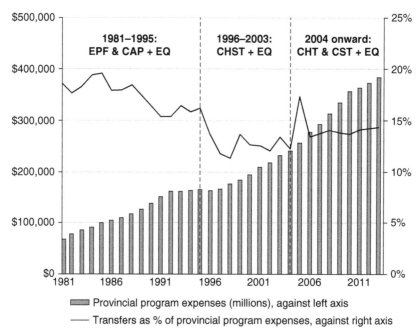

Source: Statistics Canada CANSIM, *Table 380–0080: Revenue, Expenditure and Budgetary Balance—General Governments.*

The declining federal contribution has been due to several historical factors, including economic recessions and an increasing public debt, particularly in the 1980s and 1990s. Given the trend of the declining federal share in program expenses, it becomes important to ensure a fair distribution of federal transfers among provinces.

The distributional impacts of the major changes in federal transfers

In addition to transferring revenue to reduce the vertical fiscal gap, federal transfers have a more important joint objective: to ensure that provinces and territories have reasonably comparable revenue levels so they can provide reasonably comparable levels of public services. The distributive impacts of federal transfers are mainly through the equalization program, but a horizontal redistribution function known as "associated equalization" was also embedded in the allocation of health and social transfers after the introduction of the EPF in 1977. The embedded horizontal redistribution in health and social transfers was not as obvious as that in the equalization program, but the specific-purpose transfers also generated substantial redistribution of revenues among provinces (see the next section for details).

As Figure 4.7 shows, because of the equalization program, the Atlantic provinces and Manitoba received a much larger and fast growing per capita federal cash transfer payment compared with the other provinces, except for Newfoundland and Labrador after 2006, when the offshore oil boom affected federal-provincial fiscal arrangements. In 2013, transfers to the Maritimes and Manitoba ranged from between $3,200 and $4,300. In contrast, the per capita federal transfer payment received by the other provinces, including the equalization-receiving Quebec, has been relatively lower and largely between $500 and $1500.

While the distribution of per capita federal cash transfers among the provinces suggests a distribution quite favourable to the four Atlantic provinces, as a group, these provinces constitute less than 10 per cent of the Canadian population. As well, the aggregate amount of federal transfer payments to this region represents only about 20 per cent of total federal transfer payments (see Figure 4.8). Due to the population size of Québec and Ontario, the largest single-province share of total federal transfer

Figure 4.7 Per capita federal cash transfer payments, by province, 1981–2009

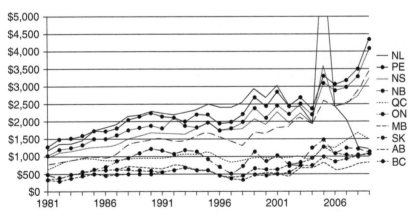

Note: The spike for NL in 2005 indicated a per capita federal transfer payment of $6,760. The spike was due to the 2005 Offshore Arrangement signed between the federal government and NL, which included an upfront payment of $2 billion made in 2005 (Department of Finance Canada 2015).
Source: Statistics Canada CANSIM, *Table 384–0011: Intergovernmental Transfers, Provincial Economic Account* and *Table 384–0004, Government Sector Revenue and Expenditure, Provincial Economic Accounts.*

Figure 4.8 Percentage share of federal cash transfers of each major region, 1981–2009

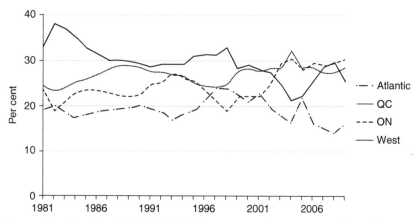

Source: Statistics Canada CANSIM, *Table 384–0011: Intergovernmental Transfers, Provincial Economic Account.*

payments goes to these two provinces, each of which took about 30 per cent of the national pool of federal transfer payments in 2009. This observation is an interesting check on the popular impression that Québec is the largest beneficiary of federal transfers due to its long status as an equalization-receiving province (see Chapter 3). In fact, Ontario also benefits substantially from the federal transfers, and did so particularly after 2008, when its economy slowed down.

Current challenges and future directions

The CST and CHT underwent major reforms in 2007 and 2014, respectively, reforms that changed the aggregate size of federal transfers and the allocation of transfers among provinces. We now analyze the effects of these changes on the vertical and horizontal fiscal gap. Based on this analysis, we suggest a few future directions for the design of federal transfers.

In 2006, the newly elected Conservative government led by Stephen Harper introduced its policy of "open federalism" and expressed its desire to have the provinces take more responsibility and accountability for health care. In 2007, the CST removed the embedded "associated equalization" component and moved to a pure per capita cash formula. The legislated annual escalator for the CST was also fixed at 3 per cent until 2024.

In December 2011, the federal government surprised the country with a unilateral decision to change the CHT. Most media attention focused on the change to the annual escalator, which was legislated to move (as of 2017–18) from 6 per cent to a floor of 3 per cent based on a three-year moving average of the nominal gross domestic product (GDP) growth rate. The government also passed legislation to replace the previously equalized CHT formula with an equal per capita cash formula in 2014–15, a change that fundamentally altered the distribution of transfers among provinces (Marchildon and Mou 2014).

The size and distribution of the CHT and CST and the aggregate impacts of all the federal transfers were substantially influenced by the changes to the CST in 2007 and, more important, by the changes to the CHT that began in 2014. For this reason, we next summarize how these changes to the CHT affect the two joint policy objectives of federal transfers.

The impact of the reduction in the CHT escalator on the vertical fiscal gap

The slower growth of the CHT, which was legislated in 2011 but began in 2017–18, means that the total size of federal transfers will become much smaller. Figure 4.9 below illustrates the share of the legislated total amount of federal transfers in projected total program expenses of the 10 provinces in various scenarios from 2014–15 to 2024–25—the 10 years during

Figure 4.9 The implication of lowered CHT annual escalator

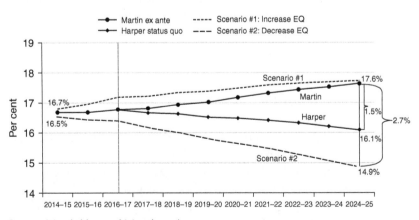

Source: Marchildon and Mou (2013).

which the Harper government's revised CHT is scheduled to apply unless changes occur.

Figure 4.9 shows that, if no changes are made to the other federal transfers, the lowered annual escalator for the CHT will lead to smaller shares relative to total program expenditures to provincial program expenses—16.1 per cent (see scenario "Harper status quo") compared with 17.6 per cent in the scenario that maintain the 6 per cent CHT escalator, as in Martin's 10-year plan (see scenario "Martin ex ante"). This lowered federal contribution means the fiscal burden of financing health care and other social programs will increasingly be borne by the provinces. In other words, the fiscal position of Ottawa will become more sustainable while the fiscal position of the provinces as a group will deteriorate.

During the 2015 federal election, Liberal leader Justin Trudeau pledged to renegotiate the CHT with the provinces. "We're also committing to sit down with the provinces immediately to start negotiating the future of the Canada Health Transfer, the Canada health accords. We need to make sure that the federal government is once again a leader" (Curry 2015). He promised to increase health spending by $3 billion over four years but has not committed to maintaining the 6 per cent increases in the CHT after 2016–17.

Although the Liberal government had not officially offered additional funding for health care in its first budget, the provincial governments put considerable pressure on the federal government to increase federal support for health care and revise the CHT allocation formula. Given the strong demand for larger federal support and the difficult fiscal situations in less well-off provinces, the federal government could consider the option of increasing the funding pool of the equalization program. For example, as shown by Figure 4.9, if the quantum of equalization program spending were increased by 3 per cent on top of the nominal GDP growth rate ("Scenario #1"), by 2024–25, the total federal contribution to provincial program expenses would be restored to the contribution ratio equivalent to the one that would have been reached under the Martin CHT. If, however, for some reason, the annual escalator of equalization program spending were to be decreased by 3 per cent from the nominal GDP growth rate ("Scenario #2"), the share of federal transfers to provincial program expenses would drop to 14.9 per cent.

Compared with the option of restoring the 6 per cent annual escalator for the CHT, increasing the pool of the equalization program is more advantageous because doing so better addresses the regional inequity in funding for health care while reducing the vertical fiscal gap. A larger pool for the equalization program will increase the federal share of provincial program expenses for equalization-receiving provinces by 1.1–1.5 per cent, an amount that would compensate, and more, for the reductions that these provinces are slated to experience under the Harper CHT (Marchildon and Mou 2013). The policy option is thus more aligned with the two joint policy objectives of federal transfers—reducing the vertical fiscal gap and enabling comparable services to be provided at comparable tax rates across the 10 provinces. Such a change might also be supported by a majority (though certainly not all) of the provincial governments. However, a more direct method of ensuring comparable services across the 10 provinces is to reform the allocation formula for the CHT or the equalization program, which will be discussed next.

Distributional changes to the CHT and CST

Before 2014, there was a modest "associated equalization" component in the CHT and CST, as a consequence of carrying over an income tax point transfer component from the CHST.[3] Because the cash transfer from the CHT and CST is calculated as a residual between the constant, per capita gross amount and the income tax point transfer of a province, less wealthy provinces received more cash transfers than wealthier provinces.

This method of calculation implies that the cash transfer component of both the CHT and the CST was, until changed, an "associated equalization" transfer outside of the equalization program. Although the cash transfer was further adjusted to avoid double compensation from the equalization program, it created a series of problems: 1) the CHT and CST achieved only partial "associated equalization" (based on income tax capacity rather than overall fiscal capacity of provinces); 2) "associated equalization" appeared discretionary and was not transparent; 3) this type of transfer caused anomalies that conflicted with the principle of equalization itself (Marchildon and Mou 2014); and 4) the principle of "associated equalization" made it more difficult for provincial governments to predict the amount of transfer to be received (MacNevin 2004).

Given the fundamental purpose of the CHT and CST, it was logical to drop the controversial residual "associated equalization" component. However, removing "associated equalization" from these transfers while

---

3 The tax point transfer was first introduced in 1967, when 4 percentage points of personal income tax and 1 percentage point of corporate income tax were transferred from the federal government to provincial governments, as part of the postsecondary education funding package. In the EPF in 1977, the federal government transferred a total of 13.5 percentage points of personal income tax and 1 percentage point of corporate income tax to the provinces (MacNevin 2004, 218).

leaving the equalization program unchanged meant that the equity objective of the federal transfer system was compromised. It became more difficult for the less wealthy provinces to provide health and social services of equivalent quality to those provided in wealthier provinces.

The Conservative government maintained that the restructuring of the CST and the CHT was pursuant to its commitment to restore fiscal balance (Department of Finance Canada 2014) and that part of its long-term plan was to "provide comparable treatment for all Canadians, regardless of where they live" (Department of Finance Canada 2011, December). The new formula, in the Harper government's opinion, would thus be more transparent, fair, and predictable (Department of Finance Canada 2014). In the absence of other evidence, the following quotation taken from the Department of Finance's website, last updated in 2014, seems to summarize the federal government's philosophy: "As a result of the evolution [of federal health and social transfers], today governments focus on accountability to the public, rather than to other levels of governments. This recognizes that governments are accountable directly to their residents for their spending in their areas of responsibility" (Department of Finance Canada 2014).

In fact, this was the only explanation or rationale for the change that we could find. However, since at least the 1990s, some wealthier provincial governments, led by the Government of Alberta, had been pressuring successive federal governments to get rid of the residual "associated equalization" in the CHST—and subsequently the CHT and the CST—and move to a per capita formula. Beyond the calculation that, at least in the short term, these provinces would benefit from the change was the view that the federal government's calculation of residual "associated equalization" lacked transparency.

Although there is little to no documented evidence concerning these intergovernmental pressures, it would only have been logical that, given his close affiliation with Alberta and that province's many frustrations with the functioning of the federation, Prime Minister Harper would have been made aware of these demands by the time he entered office in 2006. It seems hardly a coincidence that the intention to move to per capita financing for the CHT and the CST was announced shortly after his election.

The move from equal per capita gross amounts of the CHT to equal per capita cash transfers of the CHT has a profound distributional impact. Because the total amount of the CHT is legislatively capped by the growth rate of economy, this move generates a zero-sum redistribution of the CHT among the provinces.

Figure 4.10 illustrates the impact of the change to a pure per capita formula in 2014–15. That year, all provinces were losers as a result of the reallocation, except for Alberta, which gained a windfall of $913 million,

Figure 4.10 The implication of the equal per capita CHT allocation formula in 2014–15

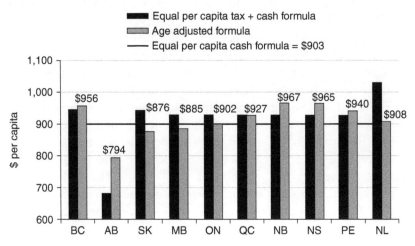

Source: Authors' compilation.

or an increase of $222 per resident. In absolute terms, the most significant loser was Ontario, which lost $340 million ($25 per capita), followed by Québec, which dropped $203 million ($25 per capita). However, on a per capita basis, Newfoundland lost the most, at $127 per resident, followed by British Columbia ($43 per capita) and Saskatchewan ($40 per capita).

The result of this change is that it makes less well-off provinces less able to provide comparable health care services to their residents. The challenging fiscal situation in equalization-receiving provinces is partially because of their lower fiscal capacity (even after the effects of equalization payments) and partially because of their higher needs for health care—the Atlantic provinces and Québec have a relatively older population profile compared with the country's average, and an older population means a higher average cost of providing health care (Canadian Institute for Health Information 2013).

On a related note, a host of expenditure needs are important to consider in the design of federal transfer programs, including differences in population characteristics (e.g., age); differences in the input costs of providing public services (e.g., labour costs); differences in cost and production functions (e.g., rural and remote locations); differences in existing infrastructure (e.g., hospitals); and, debatably, difference in net accumulated public debt (MacNevin 2004, 29–30). To address the provinces' disparities in revenue capacities and expenditure pressures and to ensure comparable public services can be provided in less well-off provinces, the federal government can either refine the allocation formula for the equalization program or modify the allocation formula for the CHT and/or the CST.

Incorporating expenditure needs in the equalization program might achieve better interregional equity and be justified by the constitutional mandate of the program itself. However, the problem with a more comprehensive, needs-based *and* revenue-based equalization program is its impracticability. The current allocation for the equalization program is contentious enough due to the very unequal distribution of fiscal capacities across provinces, especially when it comes to revenues generated from non-renewable resources, without adding further conflict about spending needs.

A more politically feasible policy option might be to move gradually to a needs-based allocation formula for the CHT. Such an approach also seems more favourable to experienced public administrators. In the interviews conducted by MacNevin (2004), a Manitoba official thought that it would be better to address expenditure needs separately from the equalization program, probably through the CHT. A Prince Edward Island official also suggested that the strongest case for incorporating expenditure needs relates to health care.

The rationale for a needs-based funding allocation formula for the CHT is that the characteristics of a population will drive its relative need for health services. Thus, a region whose population has more health needs should get a larger share of the central budget (Hurley 2004; Kephart and Asada 2009). Although there could be numerous needs incorporated into the allocation of the CHT, we suggest two factors as a starting point: the demographic structure and the geographical distribution of a region's population. As well as being important determinants of the cost of providing health care, these two factors are not amenable to policy manipulation in the short term (Marchildon and Mou 2014).

As shown in Figure 4.10, if the demographic differences in the provinces were taken into account in the allocation of the CHT, the four Atlantic provinces, Québec, and British Columbia would receive a larger per capita CHT than they do under the current equal per capita allocation. An age-adjusted per capita allocation of the CHT would partially compensate for the loss of the "associated equalization" component in the old CHT. Moreover, based on self-interest alone, it is likely that a formula adjusted for age would receive political support from most provinces. It would, however, be politically difficult to adopt an age-adjusted allocation and reverse the earlier windfalls for Alberta, particularly during a period of low oil prices.

Conclusion

The major problems associated with the federal transfer system include the lack of a cohesive conceptual basis for transfers in general. This is a consequence of the fact that scholars do not treat the equalization program and the CHT and CST specific-purpose transfers as a system (MacNevin 2004, 4). From the perspective of provincial decision makers—especially ministers and officials from the provincial treasury boards and departments of finance—this may seem like common sense given that all three transfers flow directly into the general revenue funds of the provinces and any increase or decrease in one transfer relative to another has a direct impact on the fiscal condition of the provincial government. However, this common sense is generally absent when it comes to intergovernmental discussions about, and negotiations over, federal transfers because equalization is dealt with so separately from, for example, the Canada Health Transfer. The respective federal-provincial narratives during the acrimonious federal-provincial debate over equalization in 2007 hardly referred to the Canada Health Transfer while the recent (2016) argument between premiers and the prime minister concerning the imminent reduction of the CHT escalator from 6 per cent to 3 per cent makes no mention of equalization.

In this chapter, we summarized the past and prospective policy objectives of each of the major federal transfers. We suggested that their shared policy objective is to reduce the vertical fiscal gap between Ottawa and the provincial governments while ensuring that comparable public services can be provided across provinces. We then evaluated the aggregate impacts of the federal transfers against their shared policy objectives.

We find that the current federal transfer system, shaped as it is by the particular histories of the policy domains represented by the individual transfers, has experienced some fundamental changes that may compromise the joint policy objectives of federal transfers. In particular, the recent reforms to the CST and the CHT have shifted some of the additional fiscal burden assumed by the federal government after the 2004 10-year deal to provincial governments. This has left less well-off provinces with fewer fiscal resources to provide comparable public services. To address this problem, the federal government could either increase the funding pool for the equalization program or introduce a needs-based allocation formula for the CHT. We suggest the latter policy as an attractive option because it could address the shared policy purpose of the federal transfer system more explicitly.

We are hopeful that future research might be less segmented and treat federal transfers as a system, when appropriate. This system perspective is useful because it brings together the constitutionally defined policy objectives and the economic rationale underlying the design of the transfers. This approach also accepts the reality concerning the political and fiscal impact of the major federal transfers on provincial governments.

References

Atkinson, Michael M., Daniel Béland, Gregory P. Marchildon, Kathleen McNutt, Peter W.B. Phillips, and Ken Rasmussen. 2013. *Governance and Public Policy in Canada: A View from the Provinces*. Toronto: University of Toronto Press.

Boadway, Robin. 2004. "The Theory and Practice of Equalization." *CESifo Economic Studies* 50 (1): 211–54. http://dx.doi.org/10.1093/cesifo/50.1.211.

Boadway, Robin, and Paul A.R. Hobson. 1993. *Intergovernmental Fiscal Relations in Canada*. Toronto: Canadian Tax Foundation.

Boychuk, Gerard W., and Keith G. Banting. 2008. "The Canada Paradox: The Public-Private Divide in Health Insurance and Pensions." In *Public and Private Social Policy: Health and Pension Policies in a New Era*, edited by Daniel Béland and Brian Gran, 92–122. New York: Palgrave Macmillan.

Boychuk, Terry. 1999. *The Making and Meaning of Hospital Policy in the United States and Canada*. Ann Arbor: University of Michigan Press. http://dx.doi.org/10.3998/mpub.15479.

Canadian Institute for Health Information. 2013. *National Health Expenditure Trends, 1975 to 2012*. Ottawa: Canadian Institute for Health Information. https://www.cihi.ca/sites/default/files/document/nhex-trends-narrative-report_2016_en.pdf.

CICS (Canadian Intergovernmental Conference Secretariat). 2004. *A 10-Year Plan to Strengthen Health Care*. Ottawa: Health Canada.

Curry, Bill. 2015. "Trudeau Vows to Renegotiate Health Transfers with Provinces." *Globe and Mail*, September 30. http://www.theglobeandmail.com/news/politics/trudeau-vows-to-renegotiate-health-transfers-with-provinces/article26606362/.

Department of Finance Canada. 2011. "What Is the Canada Health Transfer?" *Federal Support to Provinces and Territories—Canada Health Transfer*. Last revised December 19. https://www.fin.gc.ca/fedprov/cht-eng.asp.

Department of Finance Canada. 2014. "History of Health and Social Transfers." *Federal Support to Provinces and Territories—The Canada Health Transfer and the Canada Social Transfer*. Last revised December 15. https://www.fin.gc.ca/fedprov/his-eng.asp.

Department of Finance Canada. 2015. *Federal Support to Provinces and Territories*. Retrieved October 2015 from http://www.fin.gc.ca/fedprov/mtp-eng.asp.

Fard, Shahrzad Mobasher. 2009. *The Canada Health Transfer*. Background Paper No. PRB 08–52E. Ottawa: Parliamentary Information and Research Services, Library of Parliament. http://www.lop.parl.gc.ca/content/lop/ResearchPublications/prb0852-e.pdf.

Gauthier, James. 2012. *The Canada Social Transfer: Past, Present and Future Considerations*. Background Paper No. 2012–48–E. Ottawa: Parliamentary Information and Research Services, Library of Parliament.

Hurley, Jeremiah. 2004. "Regionalization and the Allocation of Healthcare Resources to Meet Population Health Needs." *Healthcare Papers* 5 (1): 34–39. http://dx.doi.org/10.12927/hcpap..16836.

Kephart, George, and Yukiko Asada. 2009. "Need-Based Resource Allocation: Different Need Indicators, Different Results?" *BMC Health Services Research* 9 (1): 122–33. http://dx.doi.org/10.1186/1472-6963-9-122.

Kitchen, Harry, and Douglas Auld. 1995. *Financing Education and Training in Canada*. Toronto: Canadian Tax Foundation.

MacNevin, Alex S. 2004. *The Canadian Federal-Provincial Equalization Regime: An Assessment*. Canadian Tax Paper No. 109. Toronto: Canadian Tax Foundation.

Marchildon, Gregory P. 2014. "The Three Dimensions of Universal Medicare in Canada." *Canadian Public Administration* 57 (3): 362–82. http://dx.doi.org/10.1111/capa.12083.

Marchildon, Gregory P., and Haizhen Mou. 2013. "The Conservative 10-Year Canada Health Transfer Plan: Another Fix for a Generation?" In *How Ottawa Spends, 2013–2014: The Harper Government, Mid-Term Blues and Long-Term Plans*, edited by Christopher Stoney and G. Bruce Doern, 47–63. Montréal and Kingston: McGill-Queen's University Press.

Marchildon, Gregory P., and Haizhen Mou. 2014. "A Needs-Based Allocation Formula for Canada Health Transfer." *Canadian Public Policy* 40 (3): 209–23. http://dx.doi.org/10.3138/cpp.2013-052.

Marchildon, Gregory P., and Nicole C. O'Byrne. 2013. "Last Province Aboard: New Brunswick and National Medicare." *Acadiensis: Journal of the History of the Atlantic Region* 42 (1): 150–67.

Marshall, Jim. 2006. *Issues in Equalization: A Discussion*. SIPP Public Policy Paper 45. Regina: Saskatchewan Institute of Public Policy.

McIntosh, Tom. 2004. "Intergovernmental Relations, Social Policy and Federal Transfers after Romanow." *Canadian Public Administration* 47 (1): 27–51. http://dx.doi.org/10.1111/j.1754-7121.2004.tb01969.x.

Requejo, Ferran. 2010. "Federalism and Democracy: The Case of Minority Nations—A Federalist Deficit." In *Federal Democracies*, edited by Michael Burgess and Alain-G. Gagnon, 275–98. London, New York: Routledge.

Romanow, Roy J. 2002. *Building on Values: The Future of Health Care in Canada*. Saskatoon: Commission on the Future of Health Care in Canada.

Taylor, Malcolm G. 1987. *Health Insurance and Canadian Public Policy: The Seven Decisions That Created the Canadian Healthcare System*. 2nd ed. Montréal and Kingston: McGill-Queen's University Press.

Treasury Board of Canada. 2016. *2015–16 Estimates: Parts I and II—The Government Expenditure Plan and Main Estimates*. Ottawa: Government of Canada. https://www.tbs-sct.gc.ca/ems-sgd/me-bpd/20152016/me-bpd-eng.pdf.

Watts, Ronald L. 1999. *The Spending Power in Federal Systems: A Comparative Analysis*. Kingston: Institute for Intergovernmental Relations.

Watts, Ronald L. 2008. *Comparing Federal Systems*. 3rd ed. Montréal and Kingston: McGill-Queen's University Press for the Institute of Intergovernmental Affairs.

Conclusion

Equalization is at the centre of fiscal federalism in Canada, yet this program remains one of the least understood in the country. In the previous chapters, we outlined the comparative historical, political, and economic dimensions of the federal equalization program and, lastly, we explored the relationship between that program and the two largest conditional federal transfers: the Canada Health Transfer (CHT) and the Canada Social Transfer (CST). In this short conclusion, we summarize some of the key issues we have raised, before outlining a few relevant reform options dealing with the future of equalization policy and fiscal federalism in Canada.

What we have learned

The Canadian federation features important territorial disparities linked to the uneven distribution of non-renewable natural resources and to historical patterns of economic development, featuring, for example, early industrialization in Southern Ontario. These disparities led to substantial differences in the fiscal capacities of provinces, which potentially represents a challenge for notions of citizenship and nationhood as well as for the policy autonomy of poorer provinces. The equalization program is the main tool available to the federal government for smoothing out the consequences of uneven territorial economic development in the country. From a territorial standpoint, the federal equalization program not only contributes to making Canada a more egalitarian society but also may foster unity in the country by mitigating the feelings of resentment and alienation that could be fed by large territorial economic disparities. Moreover, equalization has most likely helped federalists in Québec make the case against the independence of the province. In fact, the economic argument in favour of Québec remaining part of Canada has often featured references, sometimes explicit and other times implicit, to the equalization program as important to the financing of the province's social programs. However, the equalization program does not take into consideration expenditure needs, a situation that distinguishes it from the equalization system that has existed in Australia since 1933. Finally, despite the link between national unity and equalization policy, equalization in Canada, unlike in Australia, does not fully eliminate differences in fiscal capacity among sub-state units, and these differences are much greater than the ones witnessed in Australia.

References to national unity and a link between equalization and Québec's social programs illustrate the potential double-edged-sword nature of these transfers for territorial redistribution and national unity. In fact, the notion that Québec is offering generous social programs thanks to equalization has produced some resentment in other provinces, particularly traditionally non-recipient provinces such as Alberta and British Columbia. From a broader perspective, critics have argued that the program is an obstacle to labour mobility across the country and to economic development in receiving provinces. This type of argument can also foster some episodic ill feeling toward and within recipient provinces. The governance structure of the program, based on the principle of federal executive discretion, can contribute to this resentment because of the perceived political calculations in decision making over equalization allocation. This institutional feature of equalization governance in Canada contributed to the explicit and contentious electoral use of equalization during the Martin and early Harper years. From this perspective, executive discretion can amplify territorial conflict over equalization, a conflict that is already likely given the large sums of money involved in horizontal fiscal redistribution. In this context, equalization is likely to remain a potentially contentious political issue in Canada.

Moving from politics to economics, we see clearly that both efficiency and equity considerations underlie the economic bases for equalization payments from a central government to subnational units in a federation. Inefficient interprovincial migration, motivated by better or more public services per tax dollar in one province versus another, may be avoided or reduced with the appropriate equalization transfers. Horizontal equity may also be enhanced through the transfer of financial resources to disadvantaged provinces. At the same time, equalization transfers may also be the source of inefficiencies if they hinder economically efficient interprovincial migration or provide perverse incentives in provincial government spending. In the Canadian federation, the frequently adjusted equalization formula has nevertheless been responsive to prolonged downturns in the economies of particular Canadian provinces, including traditional non-recipient provinces such as Ontario after the 2008 economic crisis. However, long-term dependence on these transfers by some provinces, persistent inequities, and the high level of per capita government expenditures in recipient provinces raise the question of whether equalization transfers have inadvertently created unhealthy dependencies and retarded economic adjustments.

Equalization and the two conditional federal transfers (the CHT and CST) share the common policy objective of reducing the fiscal gap between the revenue collection and capacity and expenditure responsibilities of the two orders of government while ensuring that provincial governments can deliver roughly comparable public services. An equalizing component was built into the allocation of the CHT and CST before the two transfers were converted to an equal per capita allocation in 2007 and 2014, respectively. Although the removal of the equalization component made the two conditional transfers more transparent and more consistent with their specific objectives, the move also generated a windfall for Alberta at the expense of all the other provinces. As a result, lower-income provinces have less relative fiscal capacity to provide health care and social services than before this important change was made.

Reform options

The explicit goal of the constitutional commitment of the federal government to make equalization transfers is the provision of roughly comparable revenues, so each province is able to provide its citizens roughly comparable public services. The equalization formula, however, focuses only on equalizing revenues. On the one hand, this approach leaves provinces the autonomy to decide how revenues are to be used—one of the chief advantages of decentralization. However, even completely equal revenues in each province would not permit provision of the same services. Expenditure needs may vary greatly across provinces. Geographic distances (proximity to major centres), remoteness, and demographic makeup all affect the revenue needs of provincial governments for the provision of comparable services. Future refinements to the equalization program may need to recognize major differences in expenditure needs.

Another key issue concerning the future of equalization concerns its mode of governance. Here the major question is whether executive discretion is the best way to manage the equalization program and to minimize political conflict. The alternative to executive discretion would be the creation of an arm's-length expert body similar to Australia's Commonwealth Grants Commission, which has been in operation since the early 1930s. Evidence from that country suggests that this type of arm's-length governance body may have the capacity to reduce political tensions over equalization by insulating the program, at least in part, from electoral politics (Béland and Lecours 2012). Neither the federal government nor the provinces have supported this, however (Béland and Lecours 2012).

Finally, because all three major federal transfers (equalization, the CHT, and the CST) flow together into the general revenue funds of provincial governments and all three share related policy objectives, future reforms should treat theses transfers as a system; doing so offers more policy options to address the challenges caused by recent changes in CST and CHT. For example, to assist lower-income provinces in providing roughly comparable public services, the federal government could either increase the annual escalator of equalization funding or modify the allocation formula of the CHT and CST to make them needs based.

The need for greater public awareness

The federal commitment to equalization payments is embedded in the 1982 Constitution Act, and horizontal fiscal redistribution associated with this federal program is clearly here to stay. Simultaneously, equalization raises crucial economic and political issues that are unlikely to go away any time soon. Grounded in a complex and frequently changing formula and the object of limited public knowledge, the equalization program must be understood in the broader context of fiscal federalism, shared citizenship, and national unity. When this is the case, its importance for the future of Canada as a country becomes much clearer. This is why we must strive to increase public awareness and understanding of this controversial, expensive, and ever-important federal program. We hope this short book contributes to much-needed public awareness, which should be compatible with both principled policy and sound, evidence-based research.

Reference

Béland, Daniel, and André Lecours. 2012. *Equalization at Arm's Length*. Toronto: Mowat Centre for Policy Innovation.

Data Appendix

Appendix Table A.1 Percentage distribution of total equalization entitlements, 1957 to 2016–17

	NL	PE	NS	NB	QC	ON	MB	SK	AB	BC	Total
1957–58	8.50	2.22	12.36	6.20	33.31	0.00	10.22	14.60	8.61	3.97	100.00
1958–59	10.49	2.90	13.69	11.80	32.98	0.00	7.03	10.63	6.99	3.49	100.00
1959–60	10.09	2.72	12.72	11.23	35.61	0.00	6.74	10.73	7.47	2.68	100.00
1960–61	10.02	2.75	12.81	11.85	34.55	0.00	6.60	10.83	7.59	2.99	100.00
1961–62	10.18	2.61	12.77	11.71	35.29	0.00	6.52	11.31	6.93	2.70	100.00
1962–63	11.81	3.41	14.32	12.55	33.83	0.00	6.74	11.26	6.06	0.00	100.00
1963–64	12.10	3.66	15.92	13.74	33.24	0.00	6.57	11.13	3.63	0.00	100.00
1964–65	11.10	3.33	15.44	13.55	39.41	0.00	7.66	9.02	0.49	0.00	100.00
1965–66	11.00	2.99	13.79	12.55	41.91	0.00	8.58	9.19	0.00	0.00	100.00
1966–67	11.04	2.94	13.49	12.45	42.63	0.00	8.59	8.85	0.00	0.00	100.00
1967–68	11.89	2.57	13.60	11.51	48.65	0.00	7.23	4.55	0.00	0.00	100.00
1968–69	10.34	2.30	11.87	10.15	54.64	0.00	6.97	3.73	0.00	0.00	100.00
1969–70	11.27	2.30	11.40	10.36	50.71	0.00	6.19	7.78	0.00	0.00	100.00
1970–71	11.01	2.26	11.26	10.54	47.55	0.00	6.19	11.20	0.00	0.00	100.00
1971–72	11.20	2.13	11.45	9.89	48.23	0.00	7.66	9.45	0.00	0.00	100.00
1972–73	10.62	2.35	11.57	9.64	49.92	0.00	6.37	9.53	0.00	0.00	100.00
1973–74	10.49	2.24	12.50	9.83	49.56	0.00	7.57	7.81	0.00	0.00	100.00
1974–75	10.21	2.49	13.56	9.85	53.67	0.00	7.27	2.96	0.00	0.00	100.00
1975–76	10.08	2.54	13.43	9.99	55.93	0.00	8.04	0.00	0.00	0.00	100.00
1976–77	11.23	2.67	14.61	11.39	52.09	0.00	7.51	0.51	0.00	0.00	100.00
1977–78	10.81	2.45	13.29	10.62	51.38	0.00	9.19	2.26	0.00	0.00	100.00
1978–79	11.05	2.46	12.91	11.40	51.01	0.00	10.03	1.13	0.00	0.00	100.00
1979–80	10.29	2.42	12.78	9.28	52.79	0.00	10.27	2.20	0.00	0.00	100.00
1980–81	9.76	2.47	12.57	9.94	54.59	0.00	9.88	0.79	0.00	0.00	100.00
1981–82	9.71	2.43	12.01	10.13	56.65	0.00	9.07	0.00	0.00	0.00	100.00
1982–83	9.54	2.42	11.80	10.03	57.18	0.00	9.02	0.00	0.00	0.00	100.00
1983–84	10.32	2.40	11.57	9.88	56.92	0.00	8.91	0.00	0.00	0.00	100.00
1984–85	10.67	2.38	11.44	9.97	56.70	0.00	8.85	0.00	0.00	0.00	100.00

(Continued)

Appendix Table A.1 (Continued)

	NL	PE	NS	NB	QC	ON	MB	SK	AB	BC	Total
1985–86	12.70	2.61	11.60	11.74	53.04	0.00	8.31	0.00	0.00	0.00	100.00
1986–87	11.74	2.39	10.73	11.13	50.94	0.00	8.16	4.93	0.00	0.00	100.00
1987–88	12.22	2.47	11.11	10.95	47.71	0.00	11.01	4.53	0.00	0.00	100.00
1988–89	11.54	2.44	11.49	10.61	46.69	0.00	10.94	6.29	0.00	0.00	100.00
1989–90	11.46	2.46	11.34	11.32	42.96	0.00	12.27	8.18	0.00	0.00	100.00
1990–91	11.48	2.43	11.86	10.85	45.33	0.00	11.43	6.64	0.00	0.00	100.00
1991–92	11.39	2.43	11.08	12.60	45.14	0.00	11.11	6.24	0.00	0.00	100.00
1992–93	11.39	2.16	11.66	11.18	46.11	0.00	11.20	6.30	0.00	0.00	100.00
1993–94	11.16	2.17	11.02	10.35	48.09	0.00	11.18	6.03	0.00	0.00	100.00
1994–95	11.14	2.23	12.38	10.78	46.07	0.00	12.61	4.80	0.00	0.00	100.00
1995–96	10.64	2.19	12.98	10.00	49.17	0.00	12.00	3.01	0.00	0.00	100.00
1996–97	11.49	2.33	13.20	11.38	46.53	0.00	12.57	2.50	0.00	0.00	100.00
1997–98	11.22	2.45	13.37	11.42	48.72	0.00	10.82	2.01	0.00	0.00	100.00
1998–99	11.12	2.47	12.72	11.58	45.76	0.00	11.38	4.97	0.00	0.00	100.00
1999–00	10.72	2.34	11.84	10.85	48.44	0.00	11.18	3.48	0.00	1.15	100.00
2000–01	10.16	2.46	12.82	11.51	49.14	0.00	12.01	1.90	0.00	0.00	100.00
2001–02	10.24	2.49	12.75	11.66	45.39	0.00	13.21	1.94	0.00	2.33	100.00
2002–03	9.87	2.66	12.66	12.91	45.19	0.00	14.71	1.20	0.00	0.80	100.00
2003–04	8.81	2.67	13.01	13.15	43.32	0.00	15.37	0.00	0.00	3.68	100.00
2004–05	6.99	2.55	12.05	12.18	38.14	0.00	14.75	7.09	0.00	6.26	100.00
2005–06	7.89	2.54	12.32	12.36	43.99	0.00	14.68	0.81	0.00	5.41	100.00
2006–07	5.95	2.53	12.01	12.58	48.02	0.00	14.82	0.11	0.00	3.98	100.00
2007–08	3.69	2.27	11.33	11.42	55.40	0.00	14.13	1.75	0.00	0.00	100.00
2008–09	0.00	2.39	10.88	11.76	59.64	0.00	15.33	0.00	0.00	0.00	100.00
2009–10	0.00	2.40	9.80	11.91	58.90	2.45	14.55	0.00	0.00	0.00	100.00
2010–11	0.00	2.29	7.73	11.00	59.51	6.76	12.71	0.00	0.00	0.00	100.00
2011–12	0.00	2.24	7.96	10.12	53.31	15.01	11.36	0.00	0.00	0.00	100.00
2012–13	0.00	2.19	8.22	9.69	47.92	21.14	10.83	0.00	0.00	0.00	100.00
2013–14	0.00	2.11	9.05	9.39	48.64	19.68	11.13	0.00	0.00	0.00	100.00
2014–15	0.00	2.16	9.72	9.99	55.71	11.93	10.50	0.00	0.00	0.00	100.00
2015–16	0.00	2.08	9.74	9.62	54.90	13.63	10.02	0.00	0.00	0.00	100.00
2016–17	0.00	2.13	9.63	9.55	56.09	12.89	9.71	0.00	0.00	0.00	100.00

Source: Department of Finance Canada, by request, 2015.

Appendix Table A.Ia Equalization entitlements by province, 1957–58 to 2016–17 (millions $)

Fiscal Yr.	NL	PE	NS	NB	QC	ON	MB	SK	AB	BC
1957–58	11.0	3.0	17.0	8.6	46.3	0.0	14.2	20.3	12.0	5.5
1958–59	20.1	5.6	26.3	22.6	63.3	0.0	13.5	20.4	13.4	6.7
1959–60	22.1	6.0	27.9	24.6	78.1	0.0	14.8	23.5	16.4	5.9
1960–61	20.3	5.6	25.9	24.0	69.9	0.0	13.3	21.9	15.4	6.1
1961–62	21.0	5.4	26.3	24.1	72.7	0.0	13.4	23.3	14.3	5.6
1962–63	24.0	6.9	29.1	25.5	68.8	0.0	13.7	22.9	12.3	0.0
1963–64	23.8	7.2	31.3	27.0	65.3	0.0	12.9	21.9	7.1	0.0
1964–65	27.1	8.1	37.7	33.0	96.1	0.0	18.7	22.0	1.2	0.0
1965–66	34.9	9.5	43.8	39.9	133.1	0.0	27.2	29.2	0.0	0.0
1966–67	39.2	10.5	47.9	44.2	151.3	0.0	30.5	31.4	0.0	0.0
1967–68	65.7	14.2	75.1	63.6	268.7	0.0	39.9	25.1	0.0	0.0
1968–69	73.2	16.3	84.0	71.8	386.6	0.0	49.3	26.4	0.0	0.0
1969–70	95.7	19.5	96.8	87.9	430.7	0.0	52.6	66.1	0.0	0.0
1970–71	97.3	19.9	99.5	93.1	420.1	0.0	54.7	99.0	0.0	0.0
1971–72	105.2	20.0	107.6	93.0	453.3	0.0	72.0	88.8	0.0	0.0
1972–73	113.7	25.1	123.9	103.2	534.3	0.0	68.1	102.0	0.0	0.0
1973–74	156.0	33.3	186.0	146.3	737.1	0.0	112.6	116.2	0.0	0.0
1974–75	174.7	42.5	232.0	168.5	918.4	0.0	124.5	50.6	0.0	0.0
1975–76	189.1	47.7	252.0	187.4	1,049.4	0.0	150.8	0.0	0.0	0.0
1976–77	229.2	54.4	298.1	232.4	1,062.9	0.0	153.3	10.4	0.0	0.0
1977–78	278.1	63.0	342.1	273.3	1,322.0	0.0	236.5	58.2	0.0	0.0
1978–79	321.2	71.6	375.4	331.3	1,482.8	0.0	291.7	32.7	0.0	0.0
1979–80	344.1	80.8	427.5	310.3	1,766.2	0.0	343.5	73.5	0.0	0.0
1980–81	363.8	91.9	468.7	370.4	2,034.9	0.0	368.1	29.6	0.0	0.0
1981–82	426.8	107.0	527.6	445.2	2,490.0	0.0	398.6	0.0	0.0	0.0
1982–83	463.9	118.0	574.0	488.2	2,782.0	0.0	439.1	0.0	0.0	0.0
1983–84	539.5	125.3	605.0	516.8	2,976.6	0.0	466.1	0.0	0.0	0.0
1984–85	578.4	129.0	620.4	540.5	3,074.0	0.0	479.6	0.0	0.0	0.0
1985–86	653.2	134.0	596.4	603.8	2,727.9	0.0	427.3	0.0	0.0	0.0
1986–87	677.7	137.9	619.5	642.6	2,941.6	0.0	471.1	284.7	0.0	0.0
1987–88	807.0	163.3	733.5	723.5	3,151.2	0.0	727.4	299.1	0.0	0.0
1988–89	838.7	177.1	835.0	771.1	3,392.5	0.0	794.9	457.4	0.0	0.0
1989–90	895.1	192.0	885.3	884.1	3,354.5	0.0	957.7	638.9	0.0	0.0

(Continued)

Appendix Table A.1a (Continued)

Fiscal Yr.	NL	PE	NS	NB	QC	ON	MB	SK	AB	BC
1990–91	918.6	194.2	948.8	868.0	3,626.9	0.0	914.5	530.9	0.0	0.0
1991–92	874.3	186.4	850.2	966.8	3,464.1	0.0	852.7	478.9	0.0	0.0
1992–93	886.5	167.9	907.9	870.1	3,588.9	0.0	872.1	490.5	0.0	0.0
1993–94	899.8	174.7	888.7	834.5	3,878.0	0.0	901.4	486.2	0.0	0.0
1994–95	958.4	192.0	1,065.4	927.5	3,965.5	0.0	1,084.9	413.3	0.0	0.0
1995–96	932.2	192.2	1,136.9	876.2	4,306.7	0.0	1,050.9	264.0	0.0	0.0
1996–97	1,029.7	208.3	1,182.3	1,019.4	4,168.6	0.0	1,126.4	224.4	0.0	0.0
1997–98	1,092.8	238.4	1,301.5	1,112.1	4,744.6	0.0	1,053.4	195.6	0.0	0.0
1998–99	1,068.2	237.5	1,221.0	1,112.2	4,394.3	0.0	1,092.4	476.8	0.0	0.0
1999–00	1,168.5	255.1	1,290.3	1,182.8	5,280.1	0.0	1,218.5	379.1	0.0	125.0
2000–01	1,112.4	269.3	1,403.7	1,260.3	5,379.7	0.0	1,314.4	208.1	0.0	0.0
2001–02	1,055.5	256.3	1,314.9	1,202.2	4,679.3	0.0	1,362.3	199.7	0.0	240.0
2002–03	874.5	235.5	1,121.9	1,143.3	4,003.7	0.0	1,303.3	106.2	0.0	71.0
2003–04	765.9	231.9	1,130.2	1,142.4	3,764.5	0.0	1,335.5	0.0	0.0	320.0
2004–05	761.8	277.4	1,313.1	1,326.4	4,154.7	0.0	1,606.9	652.2	0.0	682.0
2005–06	861.0	276.6	1,343.5	1,348.0	4,798.1	0.0	1,601.0	88.7	0.0	589.7
2006–07	686.6	291.3	1,385.5	1,450.8	5,539.3	0.0	1,709.4	12.7	0.0	459.4
2007–08	477.4	294.0	1,464.5	1,476.5	7,160.4	0.0	1,825.8	226.1	0.0	0.0
2008–09	0.0	321.7	1,464.9	1,583.8	8,028.4	0.0	2,063.4	0.0	0.0	0.0
2009–10	0.0	339.9	1,390.7	1,689.4	8,354.5	347.0	2,063.4	0.0	0.0	0.0
2010–11	0.0	329.8	1,110.3	1,581.5	8,552.2	972.1	1,826.0	0.0	0.0	0.0
2011–12	0.0	328.8	1,167.0	1,482.8	7,814.5	2,199.5	1,665.9	0.0	0.0	0.0
2012–13	0.0	337.1	1,268.0	1,494.9	7,391.1	3,260.7	1,670.7	0.0	0.0	0.0
2013–14	0.0	339.5	1,457.9	1,513.1	7,833.0	3,169.4	1,792.3	0.0	0.0	0.0
2014–15	0.0	359.8	1,619.5	1,666.0	9,285.7	1,988.4	1,749.9	0.0	0.0	0.0
2015–16	0.0	361.0	1,689.6	1,668.9	9,520.9	2,363.0	1,738.0	0.0	0.0	0.0
2016–17	0.0	380.1	1,722.3	1,708.4	10,029.9	2,304.2	1,735.6	0.0	0.0	0.0

Source: Department of Finance Canada, by request, September 2016.

Appendix Table A.2 Per capita equalization entitlements by province, 1957–58 to 2016–17 ($)

	NL	PE	NS	NB	QC	ON	MB	SK	AB	BC
1957–58	28	31	25	15	10	0	16	23	10	4
1958–59	47	56	37	40	13	0	15	23	11	4
1959–60	50	59	39	42	16	0	17	26	13	4
1960–61	45	54	36	41	14	0	15	24	12	4
1961–62	46	51	36	40	14	0	15	25	11	3
1962–63	51	65	39	42	13	0	15	25	9	0
1963–64	50	67	42	44	12	0	14	23	5	0
1964–65	56	74	50	54	17	0	19	23	1	0
1965–66	72	87	58	65	23	0	28	31	0	0
1966–67	79	96	63	72	26	0	32	33	0	0
1967–68	132	130	99	103	46	0	41	26	0	0
1968–69	145	148	110	115	65	0	51	28	0	0
1969–70	186	176	125	140	72	0	54	69	0	0
1970–71	188	181	127	148	70	0	56	105	0	0
1971–72	198	177	135	145	74	0	72	95	0	0
1972–73	211	222	154	159	87	0	68	111	0	0
1973–74	286	290	229	223	119	0	112	127	0	0
1974–75	318	367	283	254	147	0	122	56	0	0
1975–76	340	405	305	277	166	0	147	0	0	0
1976–77	407	458	357	337	166	0	149	11	0	0
1977–78	492	525	407	393	205	0	228	62	0	0
1978–79	566	589	444	474	230	0	280	34	0	0
1979–80	604	658	503	441	273	0	331	77	0	0
1980–81	635	743	550	525	313	0	356	31	0	0
1981–82	742	866	617	630	380	0	385	0	0	0
1982–83	809	954	668	690	423	0	420	0	0	0
1983–84	931	1001	697	723	451	0	440	0	0	0
1984–85	997	1019	707	750	464	0	447	0	0	0
1985–86	1128	1050	673	835	409	0	395	0	0	0
1986–87	1176	1073	697	886	439	0	432	277	0	0
1987–88	1403	1269	821	994	465	0	662	290	0	0
1988–89	1459	1370	931	1056	496	0	721	445	0	0

(Continued)

Appendix Table A.2 (Continued)

	NL	PE	NS	NB	QC	ON	MB	SK	AB	BC
1989–90	1552	1475	980	1203	484	0	868	627	0	0
1990–91	1591	1489	1042	1173	518	0	827	527	0	0
1991–92	1508	1430	929	1297	490	0	768	478	0	0
1992–93	1528	1283	987	1163	505	0	784	489	0	0
1993–94	1551	1322	962	1114	542	0	807	483	0	0
1994–95	1668	1439	1149	1236	551	0	966	409	0	0
1995–96	1643	1430	1225	1167	597	0	931	260	0	0
1996–97	1840	1535	1270	1355	575	0	993	220	0	0
1997–98	1984	1752	1396	1478	652	0	927	192	0	0
1998–99	1979	1749	1310	1482	602	0	960	469	0	0
1999–00	2191	1872	1382	1576	721	0	1067	374	0	31
2000–01	2107	1973	1503	1679	731	0	1146	207	0	0
2001–02	2022	1875	1410	1603	633	0	1183	200	0	59
2002–03	1683	1720	1200	1526	538	0	1127	107	0	17
2003–04	1477	1690	1205	1524	503	0	1148	0	0	78
2004–05	1472	2015	1397	1770	551	0	1370	774	0	164
2005–06	1674	2003	1432	1802	633	0	1359	89	0	141
2006–07	1345	2113	1477	1946	726	0	1444	13	0	108
2007–08	938	2134	1566	1981	931	0	1535	226	0	0
2008–09	0	2318	1565	2121	1034	0	1723	0	0	0
2009–10	0	2430	1482	2253	1065	27	1707	0	0	0
2010–11	0	2328	1179	2100	1079	74	1496	0	0	0
2011–12	0	2283	1236	1963	976	166	1350	0	0	0
2012–13	0	2321	1342	1975	914	243	1336	0	0	0
2013–14	0	2334	1546	2002	961	234	1416	0	0	0
2014–15	0	2462	1718	2208	1130	145	1367	0	0	0
2015–16	0	2465	1792	2214	1152	171	1344	0	0	0

Source: Department of Finance Canada; Statistics Canada CANSIM, *Table 051–0001: Estimates of Population for 1971–2016* and *Table 051–0024: Estimates of Population for 1957–1970.*

Appendix Table A.3 Provincial GDP per capita, 2007 chained $, 1981–2014, indexed

	NL	PE	NS	NB	QC	ON	MB	SK	AB	BC	10 Prov.
1980–81											
1981–82	0.70	0.59	0.70	0.66	0.85	0.99	0.88	1.00	1.57	1.10	1.00
1982–83	0.73	0.61	0.76	0.70	0.85	0.99	0.89	1.01	1.54	1.05	1.00
1983–84	0.74	0.65	0.76	0.73	0.85	1.01	0.87	1.00	1.49	1.03	1.00
1984–85	0.72	0.63	0.77	0.71	0.85	1.04	0.89	0.97	1.49	0.98	1.00
1985–86	0.71	0.60	0.77	0.70	0.84	1.03	0.90	0.95	1.54	1.00	1.00
1986–87	0.71	0.62	0.78	0.74	0.84	1.04	0.89	0.99	1.46	0.99	1.00
1987–88	0.72	0.61	0.78	0.76	0.84	1.04	0.87	0.97	1.44	1.01	1.00
1988–89	0.73	0.61	0.76	0.73	0.84	1.04	0.84	0.91	1.50	1.01	1.00
1989–90	0.75	0.62	0.77	0.73	0.83	1.04	0.86	0.93	1.49	1.01	1.00
1990–91	0.77	0.63	0.77	0.72	0.83	1.02	0.89	1.02	1.51	1.01	1.00
1991–92	0.79	0.65	0.78	0.74	0.83	1.00	0.89	1.07	1.54	1.02	1.00
1992–93	0.78	0.66	0.79	0.75	0.83	1.00	0.89	1.03	1.53	1.02	1.00
1993–94	0.78	0.66	0.77	0.76	0.83	0.99	0.88	1.07	1.60	1.03	1.00
1994–95	0.79	0.66	0.75	0.75	0.84	1.00	0.88	1.07	1.62	0.99	1.00
1995–96	0.81	0.69	0.74	0.76	0.84	1.00	0.86	1.06	1.62	0.97	1.00
1996–97	0.78	0.70	0.73	0.76	0.84	1.00	0.87	1.08	1.63	0.97	1.00
1997–98	0.78	0.69	0.74	0.75	0.83	1.01	0.88	1.10	1.65	0.95	1.00
1998–99	0.81	0.69	0.75	0.75	0.83	1.01	0.89	1.11	1.64	0.92	1.00
1999–00	0.83	0.69	0.75	0.76	0.84	1.02	0.86	1.07	1.57	0.91	1.00
2000–01	0.85	0.68	0.74	0.75	0.84	1.03	0.86	1.06	1.57	0.91	1.00
2001–02	0.87	0.66	0.76	0.76	0.85	1.02	0.86	1.05	1.56	0.90	1.00
2002–03	1.00	0.68	0.78	0.78	0.85	1.02	0.85	1.03	1.53	0.91	1.00
2003–04	1.06	0.69	0.78	0.79	0.85	1.01	0.85	1.07	1.54	0.92	1.00
2004–05	1.03	0.69	0.76	0.80	0.84	1.00	0.85	1.10	1.56	0.92	1.00
2005–06	1.04	0.70	0.76	0.79	0.83	1.00	0.85	1.10	1.55	0.94	1.00
2006–07	1.08	0.71	0.75	0.79	0.82	0.99	0.86	1.07	1.58	0.96	1.00
2007–08	1.19	0.70	0.76	0.79	0.83	0.98	0.87	1.09	1.55	0.96	1.00
2008–09	1.17	0.70	0.77	0.80	0.84	0.97	0.90	1.13	1.54	0.96	1.00
2009–10	1.08	0.73	0.80	0.81	0.86	0.97	0.93	1.10	1.48	0.96	1.00
2010–11	1.11	0.72	0.81	0.81	0.85	0.97	0.92	1.11	1.50	0.96	1.00
2011–12	1.11	0.71	0.79	0.79	0.84	0.97	0.91	1.13	1.54	0.96	1.00
2012–13	1.05	0.71	0.78	0.78	0.83	0.96	0.92	1.12	1.55	0.97	1.00
2013–14	1.10	0.71	0.77	0.78	0.83	0.96	0.93	1.15	1.57	0.97	1.00
2014–15	1.06	0.71	0.77	0.76	0.82	0.96	0.92	1.14	1.57	0.97	1.00

Source: Statistics Canada CANSIM, *Table 384–0038: Gross Domestic Product, Expenditure-Based, Provincial and Territorial, Annual (dollars × 1,000,000)*; Statistics Canada CANSIM, *Table 051–0001: Estimates of Population.*

Appendix Table A.4 Household disposable income per capita, 1980 to 2013, indexed

	NL	PE	NS	NB	QC	ON	MB	SK	AB	BC	Canada
1980	0.69	0.74	0.87	0.78	0.90	1.08	0.88	0.86	1.16	1.12	1.00
1981	0.68	0.76	0.86	0.77	0.89	1.07	0.93	0.95	1.18	1.11	1.00
1982	0.70	0.82	0.88	0.79	0.88	1.08	0.96	0.97	1.15	1.08	1.00
1983	0.68	0.83	0.89	0.81	0.88	1.11	0.93	0.93	1.11	1.04	1.00
1984	0.67	0.80	0.89	0.80	0.90	1.11	0.98	0.91	1.06	1.01	1.00
1985	0.68	0.80	0.90	0.79	0.89	1.11	0.98	0.90	1.11	1.00	1.00
1986	0.69	0.83	0.89	0.81	0.90	1.11	0.96	0.94	1.07	1.00	1.00
1987	0.73	0.84	0.90	0.82	0.91	1.11	0.94	0.83	1.04	1.01	1.00
1988	0.74	0.85	0.90	0.83	0.90	1.11	0.93	0.81	1.06	1.01	1.00
1989	0.74	0.85	0.91	0.83	0.90	1.10	0.93	0.80	1.06	1.03	1.00
1990	0.76	0.86	0.91	0.83	0.90	1.09	0.95	0.84	1.07	1.05	1.00
1991	0.78	0.87	0.92	0.84	0.90	1.08	0.94	0.84	1.06	1.05	1.00
1992	0.78	0.87	0.93	0.86	0.91	1.08	0.94	0.83	1.04	1.05	1.00
1993	0.78	0.90	0.94	0.87	0.91	1.08	0.93	0.85	1.07	1.05	1.00
1994	0.80	0.89	0.93	0.88	0.90	1.07	0.94	0.85	1.06	1.06	1.00
1995	0.79	0.89	0.93	0.87	0.90	1.08	0.94	0.87	1.05	1.05	1.00
1996	0.79	0.89	0.91	0.87	0.91	1.07	0.94	0.89	1.07	1.04	1.00
1997	0.78	0.88	0.91	0.87	0.90	1.08	0.92	0.85	1.09	1.02	1.00
1998	0.78	0.87	0.92	0.88	0.89	1.09	0.92	0.84	1.10	1.00	1.00
1999	0.80	0.88	0.93	0.89	0.89	1.09	0.93	0.86	1.07	1.00	1.00
2000	0.80	0.88	0.91	0.87	0.90	1.09	0.91	0.85	1.09	0.98	1.00
2001	0.81	0.87	0.91	0.87	0.90	1.07	0.91	0.85	1.16	0.98	1.00
2002	0.82	0.89	0.91	0.87	0.91	1.06	0.91	0.86	1.14	1.00	1.00
2003	0.83	0.87	0.91	0.87	0.92	1.05	0.90	0.88	1.13	1.00	1.00
2004	0.82	0.85	0.90	0.87	0.92	1.04	0.90	0.90	1.17	1.01	1.00
2005	0.82	0.85	0.92	0.87	0.91	1.03	0.89	0.89	1.22	1.01	1.00
2006	0.99	0.85	0.90	0.86	0.89	1.02	0.89	0.90	1.26	1.03	1.00
2007	0.94	0.85	0.90	0.87	0.90	1.01	0.90	0.94	1.25	1.03	1.00
2008	0.89	0.86	0.90	0.88	0.90	1.00	0.91	1.03	1.26	1.03	1.00
2009	0.94	0.88	0.92	0.90	0.90	1.02	0.91	1.00	1.21	1.02	1.00
2010	0.94	0.89	0.92	0.90	0.89	1.02	0.90	0.99	1.22	1.02	1.00
2011	0.96	0.87	0.93	0.90	0.88	1.01	0.90	1.03	1.25	1.02	1.00
2012	1.00	0.87	0.90	0.90	0.89	1.00	0.91	1.04	1.29	1.01	1.00
2013	1.02	0.86	0.89	0.89	0.87	0.99	0.91	1.08	1.32	1.03	1.00

Source: Statistics Canada CANSIM, *Table 384–5000: Provincial and Territorial Gross Domestic Product by Income and by Expenditure Accounts–1902.*

Appendix Table A.5 Net interprovincial migration per 1,000 inhabitants, 1980–81 to 2014–15

	NL	PE	NS	NB	QC	ON	MB	SK	AB	BC
1980–81	−6.20	−10.11	−3.33	−7.06	−3.51	−3.80	−9.09	−3.94	20.20	13.79
1981–82	−9.90	−6.93	−2.26	−4.02	−3.94	−0.64	−2.53	−0.33	15.96	3.08
1982–83	3.19	5.15	4.41	5.02	−3.75	2.64	2.43	3.63	−4.92	−0.52
1983–84	−3.50	6.37	4.38	2.51	−2.64	4.03	0.32	2.13	−13.36	2.28
1984–85	−5.94	1.98	2.91	−0.94	−1.21	3.70	−0.56	−1.40	−8.68	−0.67
1985–86	−9.87	−0.60	−1.49	−2.61	−0.80	3.61	−2.12	−6.77	−1.59	−1.51
1986–87	−7.67	−1.60	−1.06	−2.79	−0.56	4.51	−2.53	−4.82	−12.33	2.47
1987–88	−6.09	2.29	−2.00	−2.69	−1.13	3.65	−5.35	−11.72	−9.51	7.05
1988–89	−2.88	2.95	0.60	−0.82	−1.11	0.99	−8.45	−16.60	−0.62	8.93
1989–90	−5.01	−1.94	0.66	0.23	−1.25	−0.59	−9.39	−19.07	2.24	12.95
1990–91	−1.61	−2.49	−0.18	1.25	−1.62	−1.13	−6.82	−12.08	3.53	10.34
1991–92	−2.88	−1.82	0.33	−0.34	−1.78	−1.06	−6.89	−8.46	1.15	11.26
1992–93	−5.31	5.00	0.10	−1.87	−1.18	−1.34	−4.98	−6.32	−0.45	11.56
1993–94	−8.54	4.71	−2.04	−0.90	−1.22	−0.88	−4.13	−5.39	−0.61	10.61
1994–95	−12.14	2.62	−2.96	−1.08	−1.24	−0.26	−2.87	−3.62	−0.21	7.97
1995–96	−13.11	4.75	−1.34	−0.49	−1.75	−0.26	−3.16	−2.13	2.80	5.83
1996–97	−14.53	1.00	−1.77	−1.68	−2.41	0.18	−5.18	−2.74	9.47	2.55
1997–98	−17.23	−3.06	−2.76	−4.24	−2.33	0.82	−4.64	−1.91	15.23	−2.54
1998–99	−10.55	1.42	0.22	−1.66	−1.79	1.47	−1.86	−4.26	8.69	−3.64
1999–00	−7.99	0.76	−0.29	−1.58	−1.66	1.94	−3.03	−7.83	7.68	−3.64
2000–01	−8.51	1.21	−2.22	−2.04	−1.28	1.59	−3.77	−8.35	6.81	−2.05
2001–02	−6.42	0.45	−0.96	−1.62	−0.59	0.45	−3.77	−8.82	8.58	−2.10
2002–03	−3.24	1.21	0.55	−1.12	−0.25	0.05	−2.49	−5.16	3.80	−0.25
2003–04	−3.91	1.05	−0.82	−1.01	−0.11	−0.57	−2.20	−4.54	3.33	1.91
2004–05	−7.17	−1.01	−3.24	−2.77	−0.66	−0.90	−6.16	−9.54	10.63	1.98
2005–06	−8.44	−4.63	−3.22	−4.66	−1.24	−1.40	−6.69	−7.13	13.79	2.10
2006–07	−7.97	−6.16	−4.40	−3.53	−1.69	−1.58	−4.65	1.56	9.88	3.54
2007–08	−1.04	−2.11	−1.92	−1.22	−1.52	−1.16	−3.11	4.16	4.36	3.41
2008–09	3.67	−3.86	−0.80	−0.32	−0.96	−1.21	−2.60	2.93	3.67	2.30
2009–10	3.02	0.43	0.65	0.76	−0.42	−0.36	−2.00	2.08	−0.89	1.98
2010–11	0.06	−1.48	−0.04	−0.21	−0.60	−0.31	−2.88	0.52	2.26	0.77
2011–12	1.04	−4.29	−3.03	−2.39	−0.86	−0.80	−3.41	1.76	7.30	−0.60
2012–13	0.94	−6.20	−3.72	−4.35	−1.29	−1.04	−4.00	0.36	9.93	−0.41
2013–14	0.44	−6.47	−2.73	−4.65	−1.76	−1.07	−5.41	−1.66	8.83	2.07
2014–15	−2.64	−8.50	−1.36	−3.71	−1.78	−0.64	−6.06	−2.85	7.02	2.68

Source: Statistics Canada CANSIM, *Table 051–0004, Components of Population Growth.*

Appendix Table A.6 Immigrants per 1,000 inhabitants, 1980–81 to 2014–15

	NL	PE	NS	NB	QC	ON	MB	SK	AB	BC
1980–81	0.84	1.18	1.49	1.36	2.89	6.25	6.12	3.06	8.47	8.33
1981–82	0.74	1.20	1.72	1.25	3.67	6.57	4.99	2.43	9.01	7.83
1982–83	0.62	1.12	1.09	0.94	2.84	5.04	4.32	1.94	5.77	5.36
1983–84	0.54	0.82	1.08	0.78	2.31	4.45	3.73	1.86	4.49	4.98
1984–85	0.52	0.92	1.20	0.83	2.05	4.41	3.24	2.06	4.11	4.18
1985–86	0.51	1.01	1.10	0.86	2.39	4.64	3.61	1.87	3.83	4.16
1986–87	0.62	1.28	1.32	0.94	3.79	7.44	3.74	2.07	4.37	5.27
1987–88	0.75	1.28	1.36	0.80	3.63	8.83	4.40	1.93	5.19	6.71
1988–89	0.75	1.08	1.62	1.00	4.31	9.97	4.80	2.17	6.12	7.89
1989–90	0.84	1.39	1.61	1.30	5.45	10.77	6.13	2.16	7.20	8.29
1990–91	1.06	1.14	1.69	1.00	6.54	11.19	5.74	2.27	7.03	9.31
1991–92	1.21	1.27	2.11	1.08	7.30	12.43	4.32	2.53	6.56	10.32
1992–93	1.39	1.23	2.83	1.00	6.80	13.81	4.87	2.55	7.21	11.82
1993–94	1.21	1.05	3.34	0.79	5.03	11.24	4.05	2.27	6.83	13.86
1994–95	1.07	1.50	4.02	0.90	3.72	11.07	3.39	2.17	6.12	12.58
1995–96	0.98	0.94	3.66	0.86	4.08	10.59	3.25	1.80	5.07	12.64
1996–97	0.86	1.36	3.34	0.89	3.86	10.77	3.55	1.74	4.97	13.74
1997–98	0.75	0.90	2.78	0.95	3.74	9.48	2.72	1.57	4.12	10.25
1998–99	0.68	0.92	1.74	1.00	3.80	8.09	2.89	1.72	3.88	8.60
1999–00	0.80	1.04	1.79	0.81	4.13	10.15	3.68	1.65	4.36	9.21
2000–01	0.84	1.38	1.87	1.16	4.99	12.84	4.22	1.83	5.39	9.79
2001–02	0.79	1.06	1.73	1.02	5.29	12.85	4.19	1.82	5.46	9.33
2002–03	0.61	0.65	1.34	0.86	4.69	9.08	4.24	1.56	4.36	7.79
2003–04	1.03	1.95	1.82	1.01	5.95	10.45	6.37	1.90	5.38	8.90
2004–05	1.05	2.27	1.82	1.15	5.76	10.47	6.55	2.10	5.39	9.77
2005–06	0.88	2.55	2.34	1.85	5.54	10.62	7.54	2.12	6.00	10.45
2006–07	1.01	5.35	2.89	2.17	5.91	9.12	9.12	3.12	5.89	8.91
2007–08	1.25	9.31	2.85	2.41	5.96	9.01	9.03	4.28	6.77	10.07
2008–09	1.12	12.42	2.61	2.57	5.99	8.18	10.82	5.83	7.00	9.74
2009–10	1.32	12.81	2.57	2.57	6.57	8.97	11.68	6.96	8.16	9.95
2010–11	1.34	18.41	2.43	2.64	6.73	8.00	12.97	7.18	8.16	8.72
2011–12	1.41	9.57	2.49	2.98	6.78	7.64	12.23	10.73	9.12	8.06
2012–13	1.29	5.94	2.37	2.67	6.92	7.90	10.14	9.03	9.48	7.87
2013–14	1.94	9.63	2.95	3.04	6.33	7.52	12.20	11.13	10.25	8.18
2014–15	1.60	9.14	2.84	3.70	5.52	6.53	11.49	10.09	9.57	6.79

Source: Statistics Canada CANSIM, *Table 051–0004, Components of Population Growth.*

Appendix Table A.7 Provincial government revenues (excluding equalization) per capita, indexed to the 10-province aggregate, 1981–82 to 2013–14 ($)

	NL	PE	NS	NB	QC	ON	MB	SK	AB	BC	10 Prov.
1981–82	0.80	0.79	0.70	0.79	0.93	0.87	0.86	1.19	1.83	1.06	1.00
1982–83	0.83	0.81	0.73	0.80	1.01	0.83	0.85	1.12	1.72	1.08	1.00
1983–84	0.77	0.75	0.73	0.80	0.98	0.85	0.90	1.21	1.73	1.09	1.00
1984–85	0.78	0.88	0.76	0.82	0.96	0.88	0.89	1.16	1.74	1.03	1.00
1985–86	0.85	0.77	0.78	0.84	0.98	0.89	0.92	1.10	1.64	1.02	1.00
1986–87	0.86	0.79	0.81	0.87	1.02	0.96	0.93	0.91	1.26	1.04	1.00
1987–88	0.84	0.77	0.80	0.87	1.02	0.96	0.97	1.02	1.23	1.03	1.00
1988–89	0.85	0.80	0.80	0.87	1.02	0.97	1.01	0.99	1.18	1.03	1.00
1989–90	0.84	0.82	0.78	0.84	1.01	0.98	1.03	0.97	1.14	1.05	1.00
1990–91	0.88	0.83	0.76	0.87	0.99	1.00	1.00	1.12	1.09	1.05	1.00
1991–92	0.87	0.88	0.79	0.85	0.99	0.98	0.99	1.13	1.17	1.03	1.00
1992–93	0.92	0.95	0.80	0.89	1.04	0.94	1.08	1.10	1.12	1.06	1.00
1993–94	0.92	0.91	0.79	0.97	1.05	0.92	1.03	1.15	1.09	1.10	1.00
1994–95	0.89	0.89	0.73	0.94	1.03	0.92	0.98	1.11	1.10	1.18	1.00
1995–96	0.95	0.94	0.78	0.97	0.99	0.91	1.01	1.17	1.18	1.18	1.00
1996–97	0.92	0.85	0.77	0.94	1.03	0.93	1.00	1.09	1.09	1.15	1.00
1997–98	0.91	0.80	0.76	0.94	1.00	0.92	0.99	1.12	1.17	1.16	1.00
1998–99	1.00	0.78	0.79	0.92	1.03	0.91	1.01	1.05	1.16	1.14	1.00
1999–00	0.90	0.82	0.80	0.96	1.10	0.93	0.98	1.09	1.04	1.05	1.00
2000–01	0.88	0.84	0.76	0.87	1.05	0.95	0.97	1.12	1.13	1.05	1.00
2001–02	0.85	0.82	0.76	0.82	1.06	0.88	0.96	1.17	1.40	1.02	1.00
2002–03	0.97	0.92	0.86	0.93	1.10	0.89	1.00	1.11	1.16	1.03	1.00
2003–04	1.03	0.88	0.85	0.92	1.11	0.90	0.96	1.21	1.19	0.98	1.00
2004–05	1.04	0.87	0.85	0.89	1.12	0.90	0.91	1.05	1.24	0.98	1.00
2005–06	0.96	0.87	0.85	0.91	1.08	0.90	0.94	1.23	1.22	1.01	1.00
2006–07	1.58	0.86	0.94	0.85	1.05	0.86	0.89	1.18	1.36	1.00	1.00
2007–08	1.07	0.88	0.85	0.89	1.07	0.87	0.89	1.16	1.35	1.01	1.00
2008–09	1.59	0.90	0.89	0.88	1.08	0.83	0.94	1.59	1.34	0.94	1.00
2009–10	1.59	0.98	0.91	0.89	1.11	0.87	0.93	1.37	1.20	0.93	1.00
2010–11	1.69	0.96	0.98	0.91	1.12	0.86	0.97	1.40	1.13	0.94	1.00
2011–12	1.70	0.92	0.92	0.91	1.16	0.84	0.99	1.37	1.18	0.91	1.00
2012–13	1.46	0.93	0.95	0.92	1.15	0.86	0.98	1.37	1.12	0.92	1.00
2013–14	1.39	0.92	0.88	0.86	1.15	0.85	0.96	1.31	1.25	0.92	1.00

Source: All data are from Statistics Canada CANSIM tables: for 1981–88, *Table 384–0004: Government Sector Revenue and Expenditure, Provincial Economic Accounts*; for 1989–2009, *Table 385–0002: Federal, Provincial and Territorial General Government Revenue and Expenditures*; for 2007–2013, *Table 385–0034: Canadian Government Finance Statistics.*

Appendix Table A.8 Provincial government expenditures per capita, 1981–82 to 2013–14

	NL	PE	NS	NB	QC	ON	MB	SK	AB	BC	10 Prov.
1981–82	1.12	1.02	1.02	0.87	1.16	0.84	0.98	1.12	1.15	0.96	1.00
1982–83	1.10	0.90	0.99	0.96	1.15	0.82	1.04	1.13	1.19	1.01	1.00
1983–84	1.14	0.93	0.94	0.93	1.10	0.83	1.07	1.14	1.29	1.00	1.00
1984–85	1.12	0.96	0.98	0.94	1.11	0.84	1.06	1.19	1.27	0.95	1.00
1985–86	1.09	0.90	0.99	0.94	1.13	0.85	1.08	1.16	1.23	0.91	1.00
1986–87	1.09	0.88	0.96	0.92	1.15	0.85	1.10	1.13	1.20	0.91	1.00
1987–88	1.13	0.94	0.95	0.96	1.11	0.88	1.16	1.08	1.17	0.91	1.00
1988–89	1.17	0.99	0.95	0.99	1.10	0.89	1.13	1.13	1.13	0.91	1.00
1989–90	1.12	1.08	0.97	1.03	1.10	0.90	1.11	1.12	1.16	0.87	1.00
1990–91	1.13	1.10	1.06	1.05	1.06	0.89	1.13	1.24	1.16	0.91	1.00
1991–92	1.12	1.10	0.95	1.06	1.07	0.92	1.08	1.14	1.12	0.92	1.00
1992–93	1.08	1.07	0.89	1.01	1.05	0.94	1.06	1.29	1.05	0.95	1.00
1993–94	1.10	1.06	0.96	1.02	1.07	0.93	1.05	1.04	1.08	0.96	1.00
1994–95	1.06	1.30	0.90	1.05	1.08	0.93	1.05	1.14	1.00	0.99	1.00
1995–96	1.11	1.04	0.90	1.07	1.10	0.92	1.01	1.03	0.97	1.03	1.00
1996–97	1.12	1.02	0.93	1.08	1.11	0.94	1.02	1.00	0.91	1.03	1.00
1997–98	1.17	1.08	0.91	1.10	1.11	0.91	1.05	0.99	0.91	1.07	1.00
1998–99	1.15	1.06	0.93	1.11	1.12	0.90	1.08	1.01	0.92	1.07	1.00
1999–00	1.11	1.01	0.91	1.06	1.07	0.88	1.02	0.98	0.86	1.30	1.00
2000–01	1.20	1.07	0.97	1.16	1.14	0.88	1.10	1.08	0.93	1.05	1.00
2001–02	1.19	1.14	0.95	1.06	1.14	0.88	1.10	1.03	1.01	1.03	1.00
2002–03	1.24	1.16	0.94	1.07	1.17	0.83	1.09	1.12	1.10	1.04	1.00
2003–04	1.23	1.15	0.96	1.07	1.18	0.87	1.04	1.20	0.96	0.99	1.00
2004–05	1.24	1.18	0.97	1.08	1.17	0.90	1.05	1.10	0.95	0.95	1.00
2005–06	1.18	1.11	0.98	1.10	1.17	0.90	1.04	1.12	1.00	0.92	1.00
2006–07	1.67	1.10	0.99	1.09	1.16	0.89	1.04	1.09	1.02	0.90	1.00
2007–08	1.28	1.12	1.00	1.09	1.20	0.88	1.04	1.09	1.03	0.90	1.00
2008–09	1.31	1.12	1.02	1.08	1.15	0.86	1.05	1.24	1.14	0.91	1.00
2009–10	1.42	1.19	1.01	1.08	1.12	0.90	1.03	1.18	1.09	0.88	1.00
2010–11	1.35	1.09	0.92	1.05	1.08	0.96	0.98	1.22	1.05	0.83	1.00
2011–12	1.40	1.11	0.97	1.04	1.11	0.91	1.09	1.23	1.05	0.90	1.00
2012–13	1.40	1.10	1.01	1.06	1.14	0.90	1.05	1.22	1.07	0.87	1.00
2013–14	1.38	1.10	1.01	1.06	1.16	0.88	1.05	1.20	1.10	0.86	1.00

Source: All data are from Statistics Canada CANSIM tables: for 1981–88, *Table 384–0004: Government Sector Revenue and Expenditure, Provincial Economic Accounts*; for 1989–2009, *Table 385–0002: Federal, Provincial and Territorial General Government Revenue and Expenditures*; for 2007–2013, *Table 385–0034: Canadian Government Finance Statistics*.

Index

Alberta, 23
  CHT and CST payments, 89, 104, 113
  equalization payments, 66, 89
  household disposable income, 70–72
  immigration, 75
  interprovincial migration, 72, 74, 77
  oil and gas, 41–42
  per capita GDP, 69
  per capita provincial government
    revenue, 77
  per capita provincial government
    expenditures, 79
  resentment towards Quebec, 112
  views on equalization, 26, 38, 42,
    46–47, 104
arm's length commission to determine
  equalization payments, 3, 7, 21, 27–28,
  37, 48–49, 113
Arrow, Kenneth, 54
Arrow-Musgrave-Samuelson (AMS)
  perspective of public economics, 54
associated equalization from CHT and CST,
  88, 96, 98, 103
  removal, 97, 100, 103–4, 106, 113
Atlantic Accord, 35, 37
Atlantic provinces. *See also* names of
  individual Atlantic provinces
  demographic characteristics, 106
  higher needs for health care, 105
  per capita federal cash transfer
    payments, 99
  stabilization provisions, 23
Australian Model of equalization, 2, 7, 17–18,
  21, 26–28, 43, 48
  arms-length commission (*See* Common-
    wealth Grants Commission (CGC))
  centralizing trajectory, 27
  equalization is not constitutionalized, 16
  financing of equalization program, 14
  includes expenditure needs, 111–12

Basic Law of the Federal Republic of
  Germany, 16
Bennett, W.A.C., 47
block grants, 10, 94–95
Boadway, Robin, 1, 59
British Columbia
  demographic characteristics, 106
  equalization payments, 66
  household disposable income, 70
  immigration, 75

interprovincial migration, 74, 77
loss under per capita CHT allocation
  formula, 105–6
per capita provincial government revenue, 77
per capita provincial government
  expenditures, 79
resentment towards Quebec, 112
British North America Act (1867), 12, 16

Calvert, Lorne, 38, 45
Canada Assistance Plan (CAP), 10, 34, 94
Canada Health Act (1984), 9, 93, 95
Canada Health and Social Transfer (CHST),
  10, 25, 34, 95, 103
Canada Health Transfer (CHT), 2, 4, 8–9, 89,
  95, 111
  age-adjusted per capita allocation, 106
  annual escalator, 96–97, 101, 107
  associated equalization, 4, 88, 96–97, 103
  constitutional justification, 92–93
  distributional changes to, 103–6
  growth, 88
  horizontal fiscal redistribution, 91
  legislatively capped by the growth rate of
    economy, 104
  Martin's approach, 35–36, 96–97, 107
  minimum national standards in health care,
    87, 92
  needs-based allocation formula for, 107
  per capita cash formula, 97, 101, 104, 113
  reform (2014), 97, 100–101, 104, 107, 113
  10-year financing scheme announced by
    Jim Flaherty, 40
Canada Social Transfer (CST), 2, 4, 8–9, 89,
  95, 111
  annual escalator fixed at 3 per cent until
    2024, 100
  associated equalization, 88, 96–97, 103
  distributional changes to, 103–6
  equalization dimension removed (2007),
    4, 100, 107, 113
  horizontal fiscal redistribution, 91
  minimum national standards in social
    services, 87, 92
  not embedded in constitution, 92
  per capita cash formula (2007), 4, 97, 100,
    104, 113
  reform (2007), 4, 100, 107, 113
Canadian federalism
  evolution toward empowerment of
    provinces, 27